A Note From Rick Renner

I am on a personal quest to see a "revival of the Bible" so people can establish their lives on a firm foundation that will stand strong and endure the test as end-time storm winds begin to intensify.

In order to experience a revival of the Bible in your personal life, it is important to take time each day to read, receive, and apply its truths to your life. James tells us that if we will continue in the perfect law of liberty — refusing to be forgetful hearers, but determined to be doers — we will be blessed in our ways. As you watch or listen to the programs in this series and work through this corresponding study guide, I trust you will search the Scriptures and allow the Holy Spirit to help you hear something new from God's Word that applies specifically to your life. I encourage you to be a doer of the Word He reveals to you. Whatever the cost, I assure you — it will be worth it.

> Thy words were found, and I did eat them;
> and thy word was unto me the joy and rejoicing of mine heart:
> for I am called by thy name, O Lord God of hosts.
> — Jeremiah 15:16

Your brother and friend in Jesus Christ,

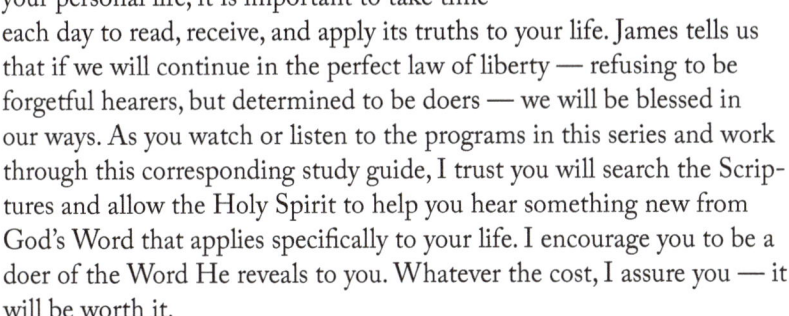

Rick Renner

Unless otherwise indicated, all scripture quotations are taken from the *King James Version* of the Bible.

Scripture quotations marked (*AMPC*) are taken from the *Amplified® Bible*. Copyright © 1954, 1958, 1962, 1964, 1965, 1987 by The Lockman Foundation. Used by permission. www.Lockman.org.

Scripture quotations marked (*MSG*) are taken from *The Message*, copyright © 1993, 2002, 2018 by Eugene H. Peterson. Used by permission of NavPress. All rights reserved. Represented by Tyndale House Publishers, Inc.

Scripture quotations marked (*NKJV*) are taken from the *New King James Version®*. Copyright © 1982 by Thomas Nelson. Used by permission. All rights reserved.

Why Christians Get Sick and How They Can Become Healthy Again

Copyright © 2022 by Rick Renner
P.O. Box 702040
Tulsa, OK 74170

Published by Rick Renner Ministries
www.renner.org

ISBN 13: 978-1-6675-0000-3

eBook ISBN 13: 978-1-6675-0001-0

All rights reserved. No portion of this book may be reproduced or transmitted in any form or by any means — electronic, mechanical, photocopy, recording, scanning, or other — except for brief quotations in critical reviews or articles, without the prior written permission of the Publisher.

How To Use This Study Guide

This five-lesson study guide corresponds to *"Why Christians Get Sick and How They Can Become Healthy Again"* With Rick Renner (Renner TV). Each lesson in this study guide covers a topic that is addressed during the program series, with questions and references supplied to draw you deeper into your own private study of the Scriptures on this subject.

To derive the most benefit from this study guide, consider the following:

First, watch or listen to the program prior to working through the corresponding lesson in this guide. (Programs can also be viewed at **renner.org** by clicking on the Media/Archives links or our Renner YouTube channel.)

Second, take the time to look up the scriptures included in each lesson. Prayerfully consider their application to your own life.

Third, use a journal or notebook to make note of your answers to each lesson's Study Questions and Practical Application challenges.

Fourth, invest specific time in prayer and in the Word of God to consult with the Holy Spirit. Write down the scriptures or insights He reveals to you.

Finally, take action! Whatever the Lord tells you to do according to His Word, do it.

For added insights on this subject, it is recommended that you obtain *Bodily Healing and the Atonement* along with Bob Yandian's book *The Grace of Healing.* You may also select from Rick's other available resources by placing your order at **renner.org** or by calling 1-800-742-5593.

LESSON 1

TOPIC
Not Recognizing Healing Is in the Atonement

SCRIPTURES

1. **Isaiah 53:3-5** — He is despised and rejected of men; a man of sorrows, and acquainted with grief: and we hid as it were our faces from him; he was despised, and we esteemed him not. Surely he hath borne our griefs, and carried our sorrows: yet we did esteem him stricken, smitten of God, and afflicted. But he was wounded for our transgressions, he was bruised for our iniquities: the chastisement of our peace was upon him; and with his stripes we are healed.
2. **1 Peter 2:24** — Who his own self bare our sins in his own body on the tree, that we, being dead to sins, should live unto righteousness: by whose stripes ye were healed.
3. **Matthew 8:16,17** — When the even was come, they brought unto him many that were possessed with devils: and he cast out the spirits with his word, and healed all that were sick: That it might be fulfilled which was spoken by Esaias the prophet, saying, Himself took our infirmities, and bare our sicknesses.

HEBREW WORDS

1. "surely" — אָכֵן (*aken*): indeed; in fact; surely; truly; verily; categorically; definitely
2. "borne" — אָשָׂנ (*nasah*): to carry, to lift, taken
3. "griefs" — יְלִח (*choli*): only translated as sicknesses, diseases, illnesses; thus, all physical infirmities
4. "carried" — לָבָס (*sabal*): to bear a heavy load
5. "sorrows" — בָאֲכַמ (*makob*): from a verb meaning to be in physical or mental pain
6. "stricken" — עַגָנ (*naga*): to strike; to lay the hand upon; to smite

4 | STUDY GUIDE

7. "smitten" — הָכָה (*nakah*): to smite; to afflict; to attack or smite in an act of war; to smite an object with the intention to destroy such an enemy; to severely wound an enemy
8. "afflicted" — הָנָע (*anah*): to be crushed; to be bowed down; to be afflicted
9. "wounded" — חָלָל (*chalal*): pierced; wounded; referring to the piercing of Jesus' hands, feet, and side
10. "for our transgressions" — פֶּשַׁע (*pesha*): sin; transgression; rebellion; revolt
11. "was bruised" — אָכְדָּא (*daka*): crushed; beat to pieces; destroyed
12. "for our iniquities" — עָוֺן (*avon*): guilt; iniquity; shame
13. "our peace" — שָׁלוֹם (*shalom*): wholeness; completeness; happiness; health; prosperity; safety; security; soundness; welfare
14. "upon" — עַל (*al*): literally, upon; placed upon
15. "with his stripes" — חַבּוּרָה (*chabburah*): blows; stripes; blueness; bruises; black and blue marks
16. "healed" — physical אָפַר (*rapha*): a verb meaning to heal; physical healing of defects, illnesses, and sicknesses; the word for a physician

GREEK WORDS

1. "bare" — ἀναφέρω (*anaphero*): to offer upon an altar; a word particularly used to picture priests whose responsibilities were to offer physical sacrifices upon an altar
2. "in his own body" — ἐν τῷ σώματι αὐτοῦ (*en to somati autou*): literally, in the body of him
3. "on" — ἐπὶ (*epi*): literally, upon, indicating the place where this took place
4. "tree" — τὸ ξύλον (*to xulon*): anything made of wood; here, the cross; a wooden altar
5. "that" — ἵνα (*hina*): points to an express purpose
6. "being dead" — ἀπογίνομαι (*apoginomai*): to die; to emerge from
7. "live" — ζήσωμεν (*zesomen*): live vibrantly; a life full of zest; same word in John 10:10
8. "stripes" — μώλωψ (*molops*): a full-body bruise; marks left on the body by scourging; refers to a terrible lashing that draws blood and

that produces discoloration and swelling of the entire body; hence, the entire body is marred, scarred, swollen, distended, and discolored

9. "healed" — ἰάομαι (*iaomai*): physically healed; to make physically whole; often used to describe a medical doctor
10. "infirmities" — ἀσθένεια (*astheneia*): an all-encompassing term for all types of sickness and disease; depicts those who are weak, sick, broken, or infirmed in body, mind, or emotion; indicative of infirmities of all types
11. "bare" — βαστάζω (*bastadzo*): to lift up or to bear a responsibility
12. "sicknesses" — νόσος (*nosos*): a terminal and normally fatal condition for which there is no natural cure; an incurable condition

SYNOPSIS

The five lessons in this study on *Why Christians Get Sick and How They Can Become Healthy Again* will focus on the following topics:

- Not Recognizing Healing Is in the Atonement
- Not Taking Time To Rest
- Not Dealing With Bitterness and Unforgiveness
- Not Putting an End to Worry
- Not Taking Good Care of Your Temple

The emphasis of this lesson:

Without question, Jesus not only paid the penalty for our sins, He also carried in His body all physical and mental sickness and disease. When God allowed His Son to be brutally beaten and crucified, He was striking a deathblow to all sin, sickness, and disease. Through faith in Christ, we have complete wholeness in every part of our lives. Both Isaiah and Peter confirm that Jesus paid the price for your total healing!

One subject that many Christians are confused about is *physical healing*. Some say it's for today, while others say it passed away with the apostles. But if we're true to what the Bible says, healing is an inseparable part of what Jesus provided through His atonement.

One reason many Christians are sick is because they don't know that Jesus paid for them to be well. The fact is, healing belongs to you just as much as God's forgiveness, peace, love, and everything else belongs to you. Jesus purchased your healing on the Cross, and you can know with assurance it is God's will for you to be well!

Does This Story Sound Familiar?

Rick grew up in a marvelous church with two parents who were very committed Christians. Going to church was so important in their lives that his dad filmed the first day Rick went to church, carried in the arms of his mother.

All of Rick's early life was spent in church. He went to Sunday school as well as services on Sunday morning, Sunday evening, and Wednesday night. He was a part of Saturday visitation, Training Union, and if anything else was happening at the church, you can be sure the Renner family was there. They were like a fixture in the church.

Throughout his childhood and adolescent years, Rick learned how to faithfully serve God. This included learning the importance of giving and developing a passion for reaching the lost. He was taught, and understood, that when Jesus died, He died for the lost and redeemed mankind from a sinful condition.

Unfortunately, the miraculous and supernatural aspects of Christian life were not taught at the church Rick and his family attended. So Rick did not understand that healing was part of the atoning work of Jesus. In fact, the denomination he grew up in generally didn't believe in physical healing. They thought that everything Jesus accomplished on the Cross was simply to redeem a believer's spiritual condition.

But eventually Rick's eyes were opened to the truth, and he began to understand the meaning of **Isaiah 53:3-5**, where Isaiah wrote about Jesus, saying:

> **He is despised and rejected of men; a man of sorrows, and acquainted with grief: and we hid as it were our faces from him; he was despised, and we esteemed him not. Surely he hath borne our griefs, and carried our sorrows: yet we did esteem him stricken, smitten of God, and afflicted. But he was wounded for our transgressions, he was bruised for our iniquities: the chastisement of our peace was upon him; and with his stripes we are healed.**

A careful study of this passage reveals that while Jesus did take all our sin upon Him, He also took our mental pain, our emotional pain, and all of our physical pain and illnesses. He absorbed it all in Himself on the Cross as we will see in the remainder of this lesson.

What Exactly Did Jesus Bear on the Cross?

Let's turn our attention to **Isaiah 53:4,** which says:

> **Surely he hath borne our griefs, and carried our sorrows: yet we did esteem him stricken, smitten of God, and afflicted.**

The words in this verse are saturated with great significance. For example, the word "surely" is the Hebrew word *aken,* which means *indeed.* It could also be translated as *in fact, surely, truly, verily, categorically, definitely,* and *emphatically.* Isaiah was essentially saying, "Indeed! Jesus has borne our griefs...."

The word "borne" in Hebrew is *nasah,* and it means *to carry* or *to lift off of someone else and take upon himself.* What did Jesus take off of us and put on Himself? Isaiah said our "griefs." This is the Hebrew word *choli,* which can only be translated as *sicknesses, diseases,* or *illnesses.* Thus, it includes all physical infirmities.

The Bible says that Jesus definitely "carried" all our diseases. The word "carried" here is *sabal* in Hebrew, and it means *to bear a heavy load.* Additionally, Jesus carried the heavy load of our "sorrows," which is the Hebrew word *makob* taken from a verb meaning *to be in physical or mental pain.* The use of these words lets us know emphatically that Jesus "bore" and "carried" our:

- **Physical sicknesses, diseases, and illnesses** (griefs)
- **Physical and mental pain** (sorrows)

Furthermore, Isaiah said, "...Yet we did esteem him stricken, smitten of God, and afflicted" (Isaiah 53:4). In Hebrew, the word "stricken" is *naga,* which means *to strike, to lay the hand upon,* or *to smite.* The word "smitten" means *to smite* or *to afflict* and carries the idea of *attacking* or *smiting in an act of war.* Moreover, it means *to smite an object with the intention to destroy such an enemy.* It is the picture of *severely wounding an enemy.* And the word "afflicted" — the Hebrew word *anah* — means *to be crushed* or *to be bowed down*.

When God laid His hand upon Jesus, He wasn't smiting His Son; He was striking the sin that was upon Him. Likewise, He was striking physical sickness as well as mental and emotional torment that Jesus bore upon Himself. These were all enemies of the human race, and God was attacking them and taking vengeance against them in order to deal a death blow.

Why Did Jesus Endure Such a Torturous Death?

Now some may ask, "Why did Jesus go through the horrific scourging and the agonizing crucifixion?" Isaiah answers this in verse 5:

> **But he was wounded for our transgressions, he was bruised for our iniquities: the chastisement of our peace was upon him; and with his stripes we are healed.**
>
> *— Isaiah 53:5*

Before we unpack the meaning of the key words in this verse, it must be noted that the healing Isaiah was talking about was not "spiritual healing" as some good-meaning people have taught. The fact is, before we surrendered our lives to Christ, we were all "…dead in trespasses and sins" (Ephesians 2:1). The word dead in this verse is the Greek word *nekros*, which is the word for *a lifeless corpse*. A dead man can't be healed; he must be resurrected. When we come to Christ and repent of our sins, our spirit is resurrected — not healed. So this verse is not about spiritual healing after all. A closer look at the Hebrew meaning of key words in this passage will reveal what kind of healing Isaiah was writing about.

Isaiah said, **"But he [Jesus] was wounded for our transgressions…"** (Isaiah 53:5). In Hebrew, the word "wounded" is *chalal*, which means *pierced* or *wounded* and refers to *the piercing of Jesus' hands, feet, and side*. Remarkably, Isaiah prophesied what would happen to Christ over 700 years before it took place.

The phrase "for our transgressions" specifically refers to *sin, transgression, rebellion,* and *revolting against God*. This is a picture of our character before coming to Jesus — full of sin, spiritually dead, and in rebellion against God. Jesus was pierced in His hands, feet, and side for all our sin and rebellion.

This scripture goes on to say, "…[Jesus] was bruised for our iniquities…" (Isaiah 53:5). The phrase "was bruised" is a translation of the Hebrew word *daka*, meaning *to crush*, *beat to pieces*, or *destroy*. And the phrase "for our iniquities" specifically describes *guilt*, *iniquity*, and *shame*. God not only made a way for you to live free from the power of sin but also from the guilt and shame that come with it.

Next, Isaiah said, "…**The chastisement of our peace was upon him…**" (Isaiah 53:5). This verse tells us the chastisement or *punishment* we deserved was *upon* Jesus. This word "upon" in Hebrew means *literally*, *upon* or *placed upon*. His physical body took our penalty in order that we might have "peace."

One of the greatest and most priceless gifts Jesus gave us is His "peace," which is the wonderful Hebrew word *shalom*. It describes *wholeness* and *completeness* as well as *happiness, health, prosperity, safety, security*, and *soundness*. It is the picture of *one whose general welfare is blessed*.

Think about it. When Jesus died on the Cross, His intention was to die for our *wholeness*, our *completeness*, our *happiness*, our *health*, our *prosperity*, our *safety*, our *security*, our *soundness*, and our general welfare to be blessed. All of this was on the mind of God when Christ was on the Cross.

Isaiah then added, "…**And with his stripes we are healed**" (Isaiah 53:5). The phrase "with his stripes" is a translation of the Hebrew word *chabburah*, which describes *blows, stripes, blueness, bruises*, as well as *black and blue marks* that are left behind from a beating.

This brings us to the word "healed" — the Hebrew word *rapha*, which is one of the very names of God. In the Old Testament, God is called Jehovah Rapha, meaning *I am the Lord that heals you*. This word *rapha* is a verb that means *to heal* and describes *the physical healing of defects, illnesses, and sicknesses*. Interestingly, this is the very Hebrew word used for *a physician*, which is why Jesus is often called the Great Physician.

To be clear, the meaning of the word *rapha* — translated here as "healed" — can only describe *physical healing*. Thus, when Jesus came and died on the Cross, He dealt with our *mental torment*, our *emotional pain*, and our *physical sickness and disease*. Not only did He resurrect our spirit through forgiveness of our sins, He also paid for the physical healing of our mind, emotions, and body.

Peter Confirmed Isaiah's Prediction

Hundreds of years after Isaiah predicted what would happen to Jesus, Peter saw the prophesy fulfilled with his own two eyes. Speaking of Jesus, Peter wrote:

> **Who his own self bare our sins in his own body on the tree, that we, being dead to sins, should live unto righteousness: by whose stripes ye were healed.**
> — **1 Peter 2:24**

In this verse, Peter said Jesus "bare our sins." The word "bare" is the unusual Greek word *anaphero*, which means *to offer upon an altar*. This particular word was used to describe *priests whose responsibilities were to offer physical sacrifices upon an altar*. The use of this word tells us that when Jesus died on the Cross, not only was He the *Lamb of God* that was taking away the sins of the world, but in that moment, He also became our *Great High Priest* who offered up His own Blood. The writer of Hebrews confirmed this saying:

> **Neither by the blood of goats and calves, but by his own blood he entered in once into the holy place, having obtained eternal redemption for us.**
> — **Hebrews 9:12**

In First Peter 2:24, Peter said, "**...[Jesus] bare our sins in his own body on the tree....**" The phrase "in his own body" means *literally, in the body of him*. The word "on" is the Greek word *epi*, which means *literally, upon*, indicating the place where this took place. The Greek word for "tree" is *to xulon*, which describes *anything made of wood*. Here, it refers to *the Cross* or *a wooden altar*.

Why did Jesus bear our sins in His own body on the tree? Peter said, "**...That we, being dead to sins, should live unto righteousness...**" (1 Peter 2:24). The word "that" is the Greek word *hina*, a word that points to *an express purpose*. In this case, it identifies the specific reason Jesus bore our sins in His body — we were dead in our sins. In Greek, "being dead" is the word *apoginomai*, which means *to die* but also means *to emerge from something*. Hence, it carries the idea of a *resurrection*.

Before we came to Christ, we were dead in sin, but we emerged from that spiritual death that we "**...should live unto righteousness...**"

(1 Peter 2:24). The word "live" in this verse is the Greek word *zesomen*, and it means *to live vibrantly*. It depicts *a life full of zest* and is the same word translated as "life" in John 10:10 where Jesus said:

> **The thief cometh not, but for to steal, and to kill, and to destroy: I am come that they might have life, and that they might have it more abundantly.**

Nearly 700 years after Isaiah prophesied how Christ would suffer, Peter confirmed his prediction. Having served side by side with Jesus and having seen Him arrested, crucified, and then raised from the dead, Peter declared: "**…By whose stripes ye were healed**" (1 Peter 2:24). The word for "stripes" here is the Greek word *molops*, and it describes *a full-body bruise* or *the marks left on the body by scourging*. It refers to *a terrible lashing that draws blood and produces discoloration and swelling of the entire body*. Hence, the entire body is marred, scarred, swollen, distended, and discolored.

Remember, what Peter was describing is not something he read about in a book. He was on the scene, living the pages of Scripture in real-time. With his own two eyes, he likely saw the effects of Jesus being brutally beaten and scourged by Roman whips all over His body. This was not just a few cuts and scrapes on His back; it was *a full-body bruise*, and it is by those stripes that we are *healed*.

The word "healed" in this verse is the Greek word *iaomai*, which always indicates *physical healing*. It can also mean *to make physically whole* and is the very word often used by Greeks to describe *a medical doctor*. Jesus took all the barbaric abuse that was laid on His body to provide salvation for our soul, a resurrection for our spirit, and physical healing for our body. The language used by Peter and Isaiah is undeniably clear — by Jesus' stripes, we are physically healed and made whole. Praise His Name!

Isaiah's Prophecy About Jesus Was Also Confirmed By Matthew

Along with Peter, Matthew also reiterated the words of Isaiah 53. He said, "When the even was come, they brought unto him [Jesus] many that were possessed with devils: and he cast out the spirits with his word, and healed all that were sick" (Matthew 8:16). Here, Matthew clearly points out that Jesus fearlessly dealt with the devil and his demons and physically healed everyone who was sick.

He goes on to say, "That it might be fulfilled which was spoken by Esaias [Isaiah] the prophet, saying, Himself took our infirmities, and bare our sicknesses" (Matthew 8:17). The word "infirmities" here is the Greek word *astheneia*, which is an all-encompassing term for *all types of sickness and disease*. It depicts *those who are weak, sick, broken, or infirmed in body, mind, or emotion*. It is indicative of *infirmities of all types*.

Like Isaiah and Peter, Matthew also stated that Jesus "…bare our sicknesses" (Matthew 8:17). In Greek, the word "bare" here is *bastadzo*, which means *to lift up* or *to bear a responsibility*. Jesus understood that part of His God-given assignment and responsibility was to take and bear upon Himself as the Lamb of God the penalty for all sicknesses and diseases to be eliminated from God's people.

The word "sicknesses" is the remarkable Greek word *nosos*, which describes *a terminal and normally fatal condition for which there is no natural cure*. This word indicates an incurable condition. Thus, Jesus didn't just come to take away our headaches and hangnails. He came and bore the responsibility of removing all our diseases — even the terminal illnesses for which medical science has no natural cure.

Just as Jesus willfully took our sins and died on the Cross in our place, He also willfully took our sicknesses and pains on Himself when the Roman soldiers tied Him to the scourging post and laid those lashes across His body. Friend, Jesus paid the price for your total healing!

STUDY QUESTIONS

Study to shew thyself approved unto God, a workman that needeth not to be ashamed, rightly dividing the word of truth.
— 2 Timothy 2:15

1. Have you ever heard Isaiah 53:3-5 explained in such detail? What stands out to you the most from all that you learned in this passage?
2. When God struck down sickness, disease, and pain in Jesus, He did it to defeat them forever so that we could have *complete wholeness* in every area of our lives. What else did Jesus defeat and provide you through His death on the Cross and His resurrection? Consider these verses:
   - Colossians 1:13,14; 2:13-15
   - Hebrews 2:14,15

- John 16:33; First John 5:4
- First Corinthians 1:30
- Second Corinthians 5:21
- Galatians 3:13,14,29

PRACTICAL APPLICATION

> But be ye doers of the word, and not hearers only,
> deceiving your own selves.
> —James 1:22

1. Did you grow up in an atmosphere where God's supernatural power was taught and celebrated, or was it ignored and rejected? How did that experience shape your view of His healing?
2. How does knowing that Jesus literally paid for your physical, mental, and emotional healing expand your understanding of His sacrifice and change the way you pray?
3. Prior to this lesson, what did you know about the meaning of *shalom* (peace)? In light of the fact that it includes *wholeness* and *completeness* as well as *happiness, health, prosperity, safety, security,* and *soundness,* what aspects of *shalom* are you experiencing? Which one(s) are you lacking and need most right now?

LESSON 2

TOPIC

Not Taking Time To Rest

SCRIPTURES

1. **Isaiah 53:4,5** — Surely he hath borne our griefs, and carried our sorrows: yet we did esteem him stricken, smitten of God, and afflicted. But he was wounded for our transgressions, he was bruised for our iniquities: the chastisement of our peace was upon him; and with his stripes we are healed.
2. **Genesis 2:1-3** — Thus the heavens and the earth were finished, and all the host of them. And on the seventh day God ended his work

which he had made; and he rested on the seventh day from all his work which he had made. And God blessed the seventh day, and sanctified it: because that in it he had rested from all his work which God created and made.
3. **Hebrews 4:9** — There remaineth therefore a rest to the people of God.
4. **2 Thessalonians 1:7** — And to you who are troubled rest with us....

HEBREW & GREEK WORDS

1. "finished his work" — כָּלָה (*kalah*): to complete; to consummate; to finish; to be done
2. "rested" — תָּבַשׁ (*shabbat*): to cease from activity connected to work; to desist from labor; to celebrate; precisely the Hebrew word used today for the sabbath
3. "sanctified" — קָדַשׁ (*qadash*): to set apart; to consecrate; to dedicate; to make holy; to honor; sacred; not to be treated as anything else; in this case, a day set apart, consecrated, dedicated; special and celebrated
4. "rest" — σαββατισμός (*sabbatismos*): sabbath-rest; a blessed rest from one's labors; the seventh day of each week, a sacred festival on which the Israelites were required to abstain from all work
5. "to the people of God" — τῷ λαῷ τοῦ Θεοῦ (*to lao tou theou*): originally Old Testament people, but in the New Testament it depicts Christians as well; all of God's people
6. "troubled" — θλίβω (*thlibo*): to rub together; to rub the wrong way; friction; constriction; pressed together; to be put in a hard, narrow, and right place; the root of θλῖψις (*thlipsis*), great pressure; crushing pressure; to suffocate; pressure to conform; a horribly tight, life-threatening squeeze
7. "rest" — ἄνεσις (*anesis*): to let up, to relax, to stop being stressed, or to find relief; used in the secular Greek world to denote the release of a bowstring that has been under great pressure; used figuratively to mean relaxation from the stresses of life and freedom to have a little recreation; relief from the constant stress a person or group of individuals has undergone; to let something go, to shake it off, or to relax

SYNOPSIS

In our first lesson, we learned one of the greatest reasons Christians get sick and stay sick is because many people simply don't know that physical

Why Christians Get Sick | 15

healing was paid for by Jesus on the Cross. Just as His atonement provided forgiveness for our sin, it also supplies us with healing for our bodies. Christ not only absorbed the penalty for our wrong in His flesh, He also absorbed every form of sickness, disease, and disorder that affects the body, mind, and emotions.

Another major reason Christians get sick is because they don't take enough time to rest and be refreshed. All work and no rest wears us out mentally, emotionally, and physically and makes us highly susceptible to sickness and stress-related health issues. But if we'll receive God's gift of rest and honor the principle of the Sabbath, we'll be regularly renewed and reinvigorated in every area of our lives.

The emphasis of this lesson:

A major reason why Christians get sick is because they don't take enough time to rest and relax. If we disregard the principle of the Sabbath, we make ourselves vulnerable to disease and a variety of stress-induced disorders. But if we'll take time off from all work-related activity one day a week and do something enjoyable, God's peace and health will begin to permeate every area of our lives.

A REVIEW OF LESSON 1

Isaiah Vividly Described What Jesus Endured on the Cross

Understanding the meaning of the words in Isaiah 53:3-5 (and 1 Peter 2:24) is vital in order to really know that Jesus did indeed purchase our healing on the Cross. Isaiah said, "Surely he [Jesus] hath borne our griefs, and carried our sorrows: yet we did esteem him stricken, smitten of God, and afflicted" (Isaiah 53:4).

We saw that the word **"surely"** is the Hebrew word *aken*, which means *indeed, emphatically, verily,* or *categorically*. It is the equivalent of saying, "Without a shadow of a doubt...."

Then Isaiah said, "[Jesus] hath borne our griefs..." (Isaiah 53:4). The word **"borne"** in Hebrew means *to carry*, and the word for **"griefs"** is *choli*, which can only be translated as *sicknesses*, *diseases*, or *illnesses*. Thus, Jesus lifted all sickness and disease off of us and took it upon himself.

Jesus also "…carried our sorrows…" (Isaiah 53:4). The word **"carried"** here is *sabal* in Hebrew, which means *to bear a heavy load*, and the word **"sorrows"** is the Hebrew word *makob*, which means *to be in physical or mental pain*. Hence, Jesus carried our heavy load of mental anguish and physical pain.

Isaiah continued, saying, "…Yet we did esteem him stricken, smitten of God, and afflicted" (Isaiah 53:4). In Hebrew, the word **"stricken"** means *to strike* or *to smite*, and the word **"smitten"** means *to smite* or *to afflict* and carries the idea of *attacking* or *striking an enemy with the intention to destroy him*. And the word **"afflicted"** — the Hebrew word *anah* — means *to be crushed* or *to be bowed down*.

When God laid His hand upon Jesus, He wasn't really striking and smiting His Son; He was striking and attacking sin and sickness as well as mental and emotional torment. Indeed, God dealt an annihilating death blow to all the enemy's devices through Jesus' matchless sacrifice.

It Was for Our Sake That Christ Suffered

The Bible says, "But he [Jesus] was wounded for our transgressions…" (Isaiah 53:5). In Hebrew, the word **"wounded"** means *pierced* or *wounded* and refers to *the piercing of Jesus' hands, feet, and side*. The word **"transgressions"** specifically refers to *sin*, *rebellion*, and *revolting against God*.

The Lord was also "…bruised for our iniquities…" (Isaiah 53:5). The phrase **"was bruised"** is a translation of the Hebrew word *daka*, meaning *to crush*, *beat to pieces*, or *destroy*. The Hebrew word for **"iniquities"** describes *guilt*, *iniquity*, and *shame*. God not only made a way for you to live free from the power of sin but also from the guilt and shame that come with it.

Isaiah then wrote, "…The chastisement of our peace was upon him…" (Isaiah 53:5). In other words, Jesus took our punishment so that we could have His *peace*. The Hebrew word for **"peace"** is *shalom*, and it describes *wholeness* and *completeness* in every area of our being. It is the picture of *one whose general welfare is blessed*.

Isaiah 53:5 concludes with this powerful proclamation: "…And with his stripes we are healed." The phrase **"with his stripes"** is a translation of the Hebrew word *chabburah*, which describes *blows*, *stripes*, *bruises*, or *black and* *blue marks* left behind from a beating. Jesus was beaten beyond physical recognition so that we can be *healed*.

The Hebrew word for **"healed"** is *rapha*, which is one of the names of God — *Jehovah Rapha* — meaning *I am the Lord that heals you*. This word *rapha* is a verb that means *to heal* and describes *the physical healing of defects, illnesses, and sicknesses*.

Interestingly, both the Hebrew words from Isaiah 53:4 and 5 and the Greek words from First Peter 2:24 emphatically declare that Jesus' suffering and death on the Cross purchased our physical healing, mental healing, and emotional healing. He is our Great Physician who doesn't just practice medicine — He produces tangible healing results that make our everyday lives better.

There's No Such Thing as 'Spiritual Healing'

Many Christians have been incorrectly taught that Jesus' atonement — His finished work on the Cross — provides us spiritual healing, but you might be surprised to learn there is no such thing. The word "healed" in both Isaiah 53:5 and First Peter 2:24 categorically and without question describe *physical healing* as well as *healing for the mind and emotions*.

Realize that before we surrendered our lives to Jesus, we were all "…dead in trespasses and sins" (Ephesians 2:1). The word "dead" here is the Greek word *nekros*, which is the term for *a lifeless corpse*. The only thing that can help a dead person is a *resurrection*, which is exactly what happened when your eyes were opened to the truth of your spiritual condition and you came to Christ. The Bible says:

> **Even when we were dead in sins, [God] hath quickened us together with Christ, (by grace ye are saved;) and hath raised us up together, and made us sit together in heavenly places in Christ Jesus.**
> **— Ephesians 2:5,6**

Thus, the thorough and complete work of Jesus' sacrifice completely destroyed the power of sin and provided forgiveness for us through faith. Equally important, Jesus' atonement — the scourging and crucifixion He endured — completely destroyed all sickness and disease of the mind and body, providing health and healing for us, even today.

Are You Violating the Principle of Rest?

Another major reason Christians get sick is because they don't take time to rest and be refreshed. Like many others, Rick struggled with this — especially in his early days of ministry. Taking a break from work was just not on his schedule, and going on a vacation was basically unheard of. In fact, for the first fifteen years that he and Denise were married, they didn't take a single vacation or even a weekend off.

When people wanted to take a break or go on vacation, Rick looked at them and thought, *What is wrong with you? Why are you always wanting a day off and trying to take a break? Your work ethic certainly isn't what it should be.* Eventually, Rick discovered *he was the one with the problem* — not them. He was an out-of-balance workaholic, and once he and his family began serving full-force in Moscow, the stress and strain of nonstop ministry work eventually took its toll, and Rick became very sick.

"I went to the doctor and received medication," Rick explained, "but it didn't seem to help me at all. The truth is I had totally drained myself physically, and I had nothing left in me to help me stand up against this attack of the enemy. Because I hadn't taken time off, it eventually wore me out and I got very sick."

Like countless other well-meaning Christians, Rick was violating a principle established by God at the beginning of creation. It's called *the Sabbath rest*, and although many believe this to be an Old Testament teaching that is "under the Law," it is actually a timeless gift from God that can be an oasis to regularly recharge and renew our strength.

Even God Rested

When we look at the conclusion of God's creation of the heavens and the earth, the Bible says, "Thus the heavens and the earth were finished, and all the host of them. And on the seventh day God ended his work which he had made; and he rested on the seventh day from all his work which he had made" (Genesis 2:1,2).

Notice the phrase "finished his work." It is a translation of the Hebrew word *kalah*, which means *to complete, to consummate, to finish*, or *to be done*. When God wrapped up all of His creative endeavors, He *rested*. Did God "need" to rest? No. Nevertheless, He rested to establish a pattern and give us an example that we could follow. The Hebrew word for "rested" is

Shabbat, and it means *to cease from all activity connected to work* or *to desist from labor*.

For some people, even the thought of not working is painful or panic-inducing. But this word, *Shabbat*, doesn't mean to sit around and do nothing. It simply means to cease from all activity *connected to work*. In fact, it also carries the idea of *celebrating*, which means God wants you to have a day to just relax and enjoy yourself. Moreover, this word *Shabbat* is precisely the Hebrew word used today for the *Sabbath*.

The Sabbath Is 'Blessed' and 'Sanctified' by God

When God introduced the very first Sabbath, the Bible says, "And God blessed the seventh day, and sanctified it: because that in it he had rested from all his work which God created and made" (Genesis 2:3). Did you catch that? God *blessed* that day off. Furthermore, He "sanctified" it, which means He *set it apart, consecrated it, dedicated it,* and *made it holy*. This word "sanctified" — the Hebrew word *qadash* — also means *to honor, make sacred,* and *not be treated as anything else*. In this case, it's *a day set apart, consecrated,* and *dedicated* to be *special* and *celebrated*.

It was on the seventh day that God "rested." Again, the Hebrew word for "rested" is *Shabbat*, which means *to cease from activity connected to work* or *to desist from labor*. It carries the idea of *celebrating* and it is the very Hebrew word used today for the *Sabbath*. Thus, one day out of seven is to be dedicated, consecrated, and set apart as holy and not like any other day.

Now if we ignore the principle of the Sabbath and fail to rest, eventually we will pay a price. Think about the law of gravity, which says what goes up must come down. If a person were to disregard this law and walk off a 50-story building, they might feel like they were flying for quite a while, as they neared the ground, gravity would catch up with them. The same is true with rest. If you don't choose to take time off, you will eventually be forced to rest and recuperate due to sickness, disease, or a breakdown of some kind.

The New Testament Also Calls for a Sabbath Rest

For the record, the principle of the Sabbath isn't just an Old Testament idea — it's also included in the New Testament. For instance, Hebrews 4:9 says, "There remaineth therefore a rest to the people of God." The word "rest" here is the Greek word *sabbatismos*, which means *sabbath-rest*. It describes *a blessed rest from one's labors*, which means God wants you to be blessed as you rest from working. This day was *the seventh day of each week, a sacred festival on which the Israelites were required to abstain from all work.*

Notice the phrase "to the people of God" in Hebrews 4:9. This is a translation of the Greek words *to lao tou theou*, which originally indicated Old Testament followers of God, but in the New Testament, it depicts Christians as well; it includes all of God's people. This phrase leaves no doubt that God's law of "rest" applies to all of God's people, then and now.

Now you may be thinking, *I just don't see how I could possibly take time off. There's just too much that needs to be done and no let-up in sight from the constant, everyday grind of what I'm doing.* Unfortunately, this is what many Christians believe, and it has produced an imbalanced, out-of-shape, exhausted group of people who have become extremely vulnerable to sickness and disease due to a lack of rest. That's exactly where Rick found himself many years ago while serving in a rapidly growing ministry in Moscow.

In the midst of unprecedented pressure, Denise urged Rick to take some time off so that he could clear his mind and rest. "Get away for a while," she urged him, "Let God speak to you and give you His perspective. When you come back, you'll see and know exactly what we need to do."

"This is not the time for a vacation," Rick responded. "I am not so irresponsible that I would take time off when we're in such a serious situation." Thankfully, he was spending time with God and reading the Word, and on one particular morning, he came across a New Testament verse that jumped off the page. It said:

And to you who are troubled rest with us….
— 2 Thessalonians 1:7

The apostle Paul had written this instruction to the believers in Thessalonica who were experiencing an onslaught of persecution at the hands of pagans and Jews who didn't support the emergence of the new church. Knowing that they were under such intense pressure, Paul said, "And to you who are troubled rest with us…" (2 Thessalonians 1:7).

In Greek, the word "troubled" is the word *thlibo*, which means *to rub together* or *to rub the wrong way*. It actually describes *friction* or *constriction* and carries the idea of being *pressed together*. It depicts *being put in a hard, narrow, and tight place*. It is taken from the root word *thlipsis*, which describes *great pressure* or *crushing pressure*. The use of *thlibo* in this verse shows us that the pressure for the church to conform was *a horribly tight, suffocating, life-threatening squeeze*. This is what believers at the church in Thessalonica were experiencing, and it seemed it would never end. That's why Paul said, "…Rest with us…" (2 Thessalonians 1:7).

This word "rest" is the Greek word *anesis*, which means *to let up, to relax, to stop being stressed*, or *to find relief*. It was used in the secular Greek world to denote the release of a bowstring that had been under great pressure. It was also used figuratively to depict *relaxation from the stresses of life and freedom to have a little recreation*. In this verse, *anesis*, or "rest," indicates *relief from the constant stress a person or group of individuals has undergone*. It also conveys the idea of *letting something go, shaking something off*, or *relaxing*. That is what Paul was urging the believers in Thessalonica to do.

Taking into account the original Greek meaning, here is the *Renner Interpretive Version* (*RIV*) of 2 Thessalonians 1:7:

> **To you who are going through difficulties right now, it's time for you to let up, take a breather, and relax. We know what it's like to be under constant pressure, but no one can stay under that kind of stress continuously. So join us in learning how to loosen up a bit. Shake off your troubles, and allow yourself a little relaxation and time for recreation.**

Without question, this verse was a stunning revelation for Rick. In fact, it was just what he needed to let him know it was alright for him to take a day off once a week, shake off the weight of his work, and do something fun to relax.

Friend, all of us need a Sabbath day to rest. Without it, we deplete ourselves on all levels and become vulnerable to sickness and disease. With it, we welcome God's peace and health into every area of our life. If you haven't honored the Sabbath day and given yourself regular rest from your work, take time now to repent and ask God to forgive you and teach you how to make time for rest. Let Him show you how to begin each day resting in His presence, reading His Word, and talking with Him in prayer. Also, ask Him how to honor the practice of the Sabbath — taking off one day in seven to relax and do something fun that is disconnected from work.

STUDY QUESTIONS

> Study to shew thyself approved unto God, a workman that needeth not to be ashamed, rightly dividing the word of truth.
> — 2 Timothy 2:15

1. What's your initial reaction to God's decision to *rest* at the beginning of time? Are you surprised? Does this fit in with the view of God you've always had? If not, what new facet is it showing you about Him?
2. The Pharisees condemned Jesus repeatedly for what He did on the Sabbath. Undeterred, Jesus told them, "…The sabbath was made for man, and not man for the sabbath: Therefore the Son of man is Lord also of the sabbath" (Mark 2:27,28). What do you think Jesus meant by this statement? (Consider reading this passage in a few different translations for insight.)
3. There's one thing that is certainly acceptable — even applauded by God — to do on the Sabbath. According to Jesus' words in Matthew 12:9-12 and John 7:23 and 24, what is it?

PRACTICAL APPLICATION

> But be ye doers of the word, and not hearers only, deceiving your own selves.
> — James 1:22

1. How were rest, vacations, or taking time off seen by your family when you were growing up? What ideas or stigmas did you associate with it? Were you raised in an environment that was dominated by workaholics, or did you learn what a healthy work-life balance looks like?
2. If you've never really learned how to incorporate a day of rest into your weekly routine, now is the perfect time to start! Invite the Holy Spirit to dismantle any lies you might be believing about what it means to rest. Also, ask Him to help you find a way to honor the Sabbath in a manner that works and is life-giving for you.
3. Part of God's idea of rest is experiencing true enjoyment, which is something that many of us don't make enough time for. Think about it. What is something you truly enjoy and is restful for you? If you don't know, ask God to show you and help you create a plan to work some clean fun into your day of rest (Sabbath).

LESSON 3

TOPIC

Not Dealing With Bitterness and Unforgiveness

SCRIPTURES

1. **Isaiah 53:4,5** — Surely he hath borne our griefs, and carried our sorrows: yet we did esteem him stricken, smitten of God, and afflicted. But he was wounded for our transgressions, he was bruised for our iniquities: the chastisement of our peace was upon him; and with his stripes we are healed.
2. **1 Corinthians 11:27** — Wherefore whosoever shall eat this bread, and drink this cup of the Lord, unworthily, shall be guilty of the body and blood of the Lord.
3. **1 Corinthians 11:29-31** — For he that eateth and drinketh unworthily, eateth and drinketh damnation to himself, not discerning the Lord's body. For this cause many are weak and sickly among you, and many sleep. For if we would judge ourselves, we should not be judged.
4. **Luke 17:1** — Then said he unto the disciples, It is impossible but that offences will come....
5. **Luke 17:3-6** — Take heed to yourselves: If thy brother trespass against thee, rebuke him; and if he repent, forgive him. And if he trespass against thee seven times in a day, and seven times in a day turn again to thee, saying, I repent; thou shalt forgive him. And the apostles said unto the Lord, Increase our faith. And the Lord said, If ye had faith as a grain of mustard seed, ye might say unto this sycamine tree, Be thou plucked up by the root, and be thou planted in the sea; and it should obey you.

GREEK WORDS

1. "unworthily" — ἀναξίως (*anaxios*): unworthily; unfit; not equal to the task; carries the idea of not matching the value of the act, honor, position, or task

2. "guilty" — ἔνοχος (*enochos*): describes someone liable; indicted; or charged; a person who is held responsible for a wrong action, behavior, or motive
3. "damnation" — κρίμα (*krima*): a judgment with an adverse consequence
4. "not discerning" — μὴ διακρίνων (*me diakrinon*): one who does not rightly value covenant
5. "for this cause" — διὰ τοῦτο (*dia touto*): for this cause; for this explicit reason
6. "many" — πολλοὶ (*polloi*): great numbers
7. "weak" — ἀσθενής (*asthenes*): a wide range of infirmities; an all-encompassing term that embraces all forms of sickness, disease, and weaknesses; someone who is fragile due to ill health
8. "sickly" — ἄρρωστος (*arroustos*): to be in bad health; to possess a weak and broken condition; a person so weak and sick that he has become critically ill; an invalid; a devastating illness; to be in bad health; to possess a weak and broken condition; a person so weak and sick that he has become critically ill; comatose
9. "many" — ἱκανός (*hikanos*): a substantial number; a considerable number
10. "sleep" — κοιμάομαι (*koimaomai*): death; where we get the word coma
11. "judge" — διακρίνω (*diakrino*): to scrutinize
12. "offenses" — σκάνδαλον (*skandalon*): scandalous; an event that causes one to trip, stumble, or to lose his footing; all offenses are due to what someone did or due to what someone failed to do
13. "if" — ἐάν (*ean*): the idea of a possibility; in all likelihood, it probably will happen
14. "trespass" — ἁμαρτία (*hamartia*): to miss the mark; a failure; a fault; to mess up
15. "rebuke" — ἐπιτιμάω (*epitimao*): to confront
16. "forgive" — ἀφίημι (*aphiemi*): to permanently dismiss; to release; to set free; to let go; to discharge; to send away; to liberate completely; to irretrievably remove
17. "plucked up by the roots" — ἐκριζόω (*ekridzoo*): to forcibly rip out by the roots
18. "sea" — θάλασσα (*thalassa*): saltwater
19. "obey" — ὑπακούω (*hupakouo*): a compound of ὑπό (*hupo*) and ακούω (*akouo*); the word ὑπό (*hupo*) means under, and ακούω (*akouo*)

Why Christians Get Sick | 25

means to hear; it means to be in submission to what is spoken; obedience to what is spoken

SYNOPSIS

So far in our study, we have seen two specific reasons that Christians get sick. The first is because many believers simply don't realize that Jesus' atoning work paid for our physical healing. Just as He took all sin and iniquity upon Himself, Jesus also absorbed all sickness and disease that plagues mankind. It's no wonder King David said, "Bless the Lord, O my soul, and forget not all His benefits: Who forgives all your iniquities, Who heals all your diseases" (Psalm 103:2,3 *NKJV*).

The second reason Christians get sick is because they take little or no time to rest and recover from work. Just as God Himself rested on the seventh day, we too are to rest from all activity connected with work one day out of seven. Those who ignore this principle often find themselves sidelined by sickness.

Another way that we as Christians open the door to physical illness is by holding grudges and allowing resentment toward others to remain unresolved in our hearts. When we fail to deal with the offenses that come our way, unforgiveness and bitterness begin to take root in our lives. What does Jesus say about offense, and what is the most effective way to deal with it and avoid the trap of unforgiveness and bitterness?

The emphasis of this lesson:

A person who takes communion with unforgiveness, bitterness, or known sin in his heart is devaluing the Lord's sacrifice and opening the door to sickness. All offenses result from one of two things: *what someone did* or *what they failed to do*. The people we're closest to are the ones who can offend us most often and most deeply. God wants us to confront and forgive those who offend us, letting it go forever so unforgiveness and bitterness don't take root in our lives.

A REVIEW OF OUR ANCHOR VERSES
Isaiah 53:4,5

Nearly 700 years before Jesus lived, the Holy Spirit moved on the prophet Isaiah to foretell what He would suffer at the hands of man. He wrote, "Surely he hath borne our griefs, and carried our sorrows: yet we did esteem him stricken, smitten of God, and afflicted" (Isaiah 53:4).

The first word of this verse, the word **"surely,"** is the Hebrew word *aken*, meaning *indeed, verily, definitely, categorically,* or *emphatically*. Essentially, Isaiah said, "Most assuredly, Jesus hath born our griefs." The word "griefs" is the Hebrew word *choli*, and it describes *sicknesses, diseases,* and *physical infirmities of all kinds*, and it can't be translated any other way.

Then Isaiah added that Jesus **"…carried our sorrows…"** (Isaiah 53:4). The word "carried" means *to bear a heavy load*, and the word "sorrows" is derived from a verb meaning *to be in physical or mental pain*. Thus, the "sorrows" Jesus carried are *a heavy load of physical pain and mental torment*.

Along with bearing our sorrows, Isaiah also said, **"…He was wounded for our transgressions…"** (Isaiah 53:5). The word "wounded" here is *chalal*, the Hebrew word for *pierced*, and it refers to the *piercing of Jesus' hands, feet, and side*. He was wounded "for our transgressions," which has everything to do with the issue of *sin* and *rebellion* in our lives. Jesus was *pierced* to pay the price for us to be delivered, freed, and forgiven of sin.

The Bible goes on to say, **"…He was bruised for our iniquities…"** (Isaiah 53:5). The word "iniquities" carries the idea of *guilt* and *shame*. Jesus "was bruised" — meaning He was *crushed* and *beaten to pieces* — to set us free from shame and guilt. If you're dealing with either of these issues, know that Jesus has already paid the price for you to live free of them.

Isaiah 53:5 then says, **"…The chastisement of our peace was upon him…."** The word "peace" here is the Hebrew word *shalom*, and it describes *wholeness and completeness in every area of our lives*, including our health. Indeed, we know this is true because **"…with his stripes we are healed"** (Isaiah 53:5). The Hebrew word for "healed" is *rapha*, and it describes *physical healing of defects, illnesses, and sicknesses*. Jesus received "stripes" — physical *blows* resulting in *bruises* and *black and blues marks* — so that we could be physically healed of all diseases and disorders.

In these verses, we discover complete healing is in the atonement of Jesus. He not only resurrected our spirit, which was dead in sin, but also dealt a deathblow to all forms of disease and sickness that come against our body, mind, and emotions. The work of the Cross is a package deal. If you're a Christian and you're sick in body, please realize that Jesus has paid the price to totally heal you and make you whole. Praise His Name forever!

Taking Communion 'Unworthily' Can Open the Door for Sickness

The practice of taking Communion was first introduced by Jesus Himself on the night He was betrayed. He gave us this sacred tradition of eating the bread and drinking the juice of the vine — which represent His broken body and shed blood — in order to remember His ultimate sacrifice for us. Communion is also the affirmation of our covenant with God and with fellow believers — it signifies that we're totally committed to Him and each other for life.

After the apostle Paul shared what many have come to know now as the communion verses, he wrote this sobering warning about receiving communion: "Wherefore whosoever shall eat this bread, and drink this cup of the Lord, unworthily, shall be guilty of the body and blood of the Lord" (1 Corinthians 11:27).

The word "unworthily" in this verse is the Greek word *anaxios*, which means *unworthily*, *unfit*, or *not equal to the task*. It carries the idea of *not matching the value of the act, honor, position,* or *task*. The fact that the Holy Spirit moved on Paul to write this warning tells us that some people who come to the Lord's Table are *unfit* to take communion — their character does not match the value or honor of receiving the elements representing the body and blood of Jesus. As a result, they are opening the door for sickness to enter their lives.

Judas Was 'Guilty of the Body and Blood of Jesus'

The clearest example of a person taking communion "unworthily" is Judas Iscariot on the night of the last supper. Although he sat at the table with the rest of the disciples and pretended to enter into covenant with them and Jesus, he had already cut a deal with the Jewish leaders to hand Jesus over. Satan had entered Judas' heart and sown seeds of betrayal, and in that embittered state, he ate the bread and drank of the cup as if everything was alright. His actions were *unworthy*, and he became *guilty* of the body and blood of the Lord.

The word "guilty" in Greek is the word *enochos*, which describes *someone liable, indicted*, or *charged*. This is *a person who is held responsible for a wrong action, behavior, or motive*. Clearly, God looks at taking communion very seriously, and so should we. It's not just the elements we need to understand; we need to comprehend the meaning of the holy covenant communion represents. By receiving the bread and wine (or juice), we're saying we are in covenant with God and with one another.

The apostle Paul wrote this warning to the Corinthians because their behavior toward one another was atrocious. They were arguing, fighting, and suing each other in court. One group claimed to be of Paul, another said they were of Apollos, and still another stated they were of Christ. Between the political divisiveness and the malicious slander, the church at Corinth was a raging mess. Yet, these churchgoers were partaking of communion — consuming the body and blood of Jesus — as if everything was fine, when it clearly wasn't.

Paul went on to say, "For he that eateth and drinketh unworthily, eateth and drinketh damnation to himself, not discerning the Lord's body" (1 Corinthians 11:29). The word "damnation" here is the Greek word *krima*, which describes *a decree, a judgment*, or *a verdict with an adverse consequence*. Just as there are natural laws that cannot be broken, there are also spiritual laws we must follow. If you break a spiritual law — which in this case is breaking covenant — there are certain unavoidable consequences.

Hence, if you partake of the bread and the cup with an insincere heart that is not honoring the Lord and upholding His covenant, you bring a judgement upon yourself for "…not discerning the Lord's body" (1 Corinthians 11:29). The words "not discerning" in Greek depict *one's inability to discern, to judge, to appreciate*, or *to be truthful*. In this verse, it describes *one who lacks discernment* and *does not rightly value Christ's sacrificial covenant*.

Sickness Can Be a Consequence of Not Valuing Christ's Sacrifice

Paul then added, "For this cause many are weak and sickly among you, and many sleep" (1 Corinthians 11:30). The opening phrase, "for this cause," is a translation of the Greek words *dia touto*, which means *for this explicit reason*. Many believers were weak and sick in Corinth because they had devalued the Lord's sacrifice and taken communion unworthily.

The word "many" is the Greek word *polloi*, which indicates *great numbers*. The word "weak" is *asthenes*, which describes *a wide range of infirmities*. It is an all-encompassing term that embraces *all forms of sickness, disease, and weaknesses*. This word also conveys the idea of *someone that is fragile and must be treated with supreme care due to ill health*. Thus, Paul in essence said *great numbers* of people were "weak and sickly" in the Corinthian church because they had taken communion unworthily.

This brings us to the word "sickly," which is the Greek word *arroustos*, and it means *to be in bad health* or *to possess a weak and broken condition*. This word depicts *a person so weak and sick that he has become critically ill*. It pictures *one devastated by illness, in bad health*, or *possessing a weak and broken condition*. It can even refer to *an invalid* or be translated as the word *comatose*.

Ironically, the people Paul was writing to were the believers at Corinth. This was the same church that was overflowing with the gifts of the Holy Spirit — including the gifts of healing and miracles. In fact, there were so many manifestations of these gifts that they couldn't be counted. Yet despite the fact that people were being healed left and right, there were still numerous believers who were "weak and sickly."

Paul also said "many sleep" (1 Corinthians 11:30). The word "many" here is the word *hikanos*, which describes *a substantial number* or *considerable number*, and the word "sleep" is the Greek word *koimaomai*, which refers to *death*. It is where we get the word *coma*. Why were so many Corinthian believers weak, sickly, and experiencing death? It was because they were holding on to unforgiveness and bitterness toward each other, and as a result, they had violated their covenant with God and their fellow believers.

Paul urged them — and *us* — to examine themselves. He said, "For if we would judge ourselves, we should not be judged" (1 Corinthians 11:31). The word "judge" here is the Greek word *diakrino*, which depicts *one's ability to discern, judge, be truthful*, or *to come under scrutiny*. Hence, if we will be truthful and take a scrutinizing look at our attitudes, our thoughts, and our actions and self-correct, we will not be "judged," meaning we will not be one who has been or is presently suffering the consequences of harboring bitterness and unforgiveness.

Before you take Communion, take time to soberly examine yourself to see if you're in or out of covenant with God and His Church. Repent of anything that is keeping you from being in sync and living in unity with others. Then partake of Communion.

Holding On to Offense Can Also Open the Door to Disease

Jesus said one of the major signs that we're living in the last of the last days is that many people will be *offended* (*see* Matthew 24:10). He also said, "...It is impossible but that offences will come..." (Luke 17:1). The word "offenses" here is the Greek word *skandalon*, which describes *something scandalous*. It is *an event that causes one to trip, stumble, or to lose his footing*. What is interesting is that all offenses result from one of two things: *what someone did* or *what they failed to do*.

Since Jesus said, "...It is impossible but that offences will come..." (Luke 17:1), there will always be opportunities to be offended. When we don't properly deal with offense and release unforgiveness with God's help, it eventually becomes a root of bitterness growing in our hearts that causes all kinds of trouble for us and others.

What is the right way to deal with offense?

Knowing how crucial the issue of offense is, Jesus went on to say, "Take heed to yourselves: If thy brother trespass against thee, rebuke him; and if he repent, forgive him" (Luke 17:3). Notice He used the word "brother." This tells us clearly that the people we're closest to are the ones who can offend us most often and most deeply.

Also note the word "if." It is the Greek word *ean*, and it carries *the idea of a possibility*. It could be translated as *in all likelihood* or *it probably will happen*. Essentially, Jesus is saying, "In all likelihood, your brother or sister is going to trespass against you...." The word "trespass" in Greek is *hamartia*, which means *to miss the mark*. It's the New Testament word for *sin* and describes *a failure* or *a fault* and means *to mess up*. When someone "trespasses" against you, they mess up or do something wrong that is offensive to you.

Jesus said when this happens, you're to "rebuke him." In Greek, the word "rebuke" is *epitimao*, which means *to confront*. Then after you honestly confront your brother, you're to *forgive* him. The word "forgive" is a form of the Greek word *aphiemi*, which means *to permanently dismiss, to release, to set free, to discharge, to send away,* or *to let go.* It's the idea of *liberating completely* or *irretrievably removing something.* Basically, to "forgive" means *to let it go forever.*

Now, you may be thinking, *What if this person keeps doing the same thing over and over again?* Jesus addressed this in Luke 17:4, saying, "And if he trespass against thee seven times in a day, and seven times in a day turn again to thee, saying, I repent; thou shalt forgive him." Again, we see the word "forgive" — a form of the Greek word *aphiemi,* meaning *to permanently dismiss, to release,* or *to let go.* That's the default action we need the Holy Spirit to help fix in our brain. When someone offends us and we're tempted to hold unforgiveness against them, we need to, instead, think, *Let it go!*

It's no coincidence that Jesus said, "And if he trespass against thee *seven times in a day,* and seven times in a day turn again to thee, saying, I repent; thou shalt forgive him" (Luke 17:4). We need to hear this instruction because there are some people that have an uncanny ability to be offensive all the time. They probably don't want to be — which is why they keep asking for forgiveness. Yet, they seem to keep repeating the same mistake again and again. In cases like these, Jesus said, "Just keep letting it go. If they're sincere, don't hold on to their offense. As an act of your will, permanently release it and let it go."

Why Did Jesus Compare Offenses to the Sycamine Tree? Four Fascinating Facts You Need to Know

How did the disciples respond to Jesus' instruction? The Bible says, "And the apostles said unto the Lord, Increase our faith. And the Lord said, If ye had faith as a grain of mustard seed, ye might say unto this sycamine tree, Be thou plucked up by the root, and be thou planted in the sea; and it should obey you" (Luke 17:5,6).

Now many people read over this passage and miss some very important insights. There's a reason Jesus compared unforgiveness and bitterness, which result from undealt with offense, to a sycamine tree. Actually, there are four specific facts you need to know.

FACT #1: **In Egypt and the Middle East, the sycamine tree was the preferred wood for building caskets.** It was very durable material and did the job perfectly. The implication here is that if you fail to confront and forgive the offenses of others, unforgiveness and bitterness — like a sycamine tree — will box you in and render you dead.

FACT #2: The sycamine tree has a very large and deep root structure. In fact, it has the deepest root system of all the trees in the Middle East, making it extremely hard to kill. Even if one is cut down and reduced to a stump, the roots are so strong and vibrant that the tree often grows back.

This tells us that bitterness and unforgiveness can form deep roots down inside us, and if they're not dealt with quickly, they will be very hard to get rid of.

FACT #3: The sycamine tree produces fruit that is bitter to eat. What's interesting is that the fig tree and the sycamine tree produce fruit that is nearly identical in appearance. The difference, however, is in the taste: while the sycamine tree produces bitter fruit, the fig tree produces sweet fruit.

Wealthy people ate the fruit of the fig tree, enjoying its wonderful, luscious sweetness. In contrast, poor people couldn't afford figs, so they ate the fruit of the sycamine tree, which was bitter and tart. As a matter of fact, it was so bitter they couldn't eat the whole sycamine fruit in one sitting. They would bite off a little piece, chew on it a little while, and then come back later to bite off another piece and chew on it some more.

In the same way, bitterness and unforgiveness are like the fruit of the sycamine tree. You mentally *chew* a little while on what someone did; you walk away and come back and think about it a little more. Again and again and again, you meditate on the offense, chewing on it a little here and a little there. The more you chew on what was done to you, the more bitter your words are and the more bitter you become inside. If you continue to nurse and rehearse the offense that was done to you, it will bring a sense of poverty to every area of your life — just like the poor people who were stuck in a cycle of eating the bitter fruit of the sycamine tree.

FACT #4: The sycamine tree is pollinated by the sting of a wasp. When a wasp puts its stinger into the flower of a sycamine tree, the flower becomes pollinated and develops into fruit. Similarly, when someone offends us, their words or actions act like the burning, painful sting of a wasp. The longer we leave the stinger in, the more painful it becomes, and that pain radiates throughout our life. Friend, if you leave the stinger of offense in your heart, bitterness and unforgiveness will be pollinated and grow in your life.

Your Freedom Is Voice-Activated

Looking once more at Jesus' words to the disciples, He said, "…If ye had faith as a grain of mustard seed, ye might say unto this sycamine tree, Be thou plucked up by the root, and be thou planted in the sea; and it should obey you" (Luke 17:6).

Notice Jesus didn't say *think about* the sycamine tree or *talk about* it to your closest friends. He said SAY something to it. To get rid of unforgiveness and bitterness, you have to *speak* to them in the name of Jesus. Your voice releases your authority in Christ, and when you tell unforgiveness and offense to go, they will obey. Sometimes you have to tell them many times, but eventually they will dissipate and be removed from your life.

When Jesus said, "…Be thou plucked up by the root, and be thou planted in the sea…" (Luke 17:6), the phrase "plucked up by the roots" is a translation of the Greek word *ekridzoo*, which means *to forcibly rip out by the roots*. You can't just say, "Be cut down," because it will grow back from the stump. You have to be committed to get down to the roots, using the razor-sharp ax of God's Word. Open your mouth and demand that bitterness and unforgiveness be completely eradicated from your life.

Specifically, Jesus said to command unforgiveness and bitterness to be "planted in the sea." Keep in mind that the sea is saltwater. If you plant a tree in saltwater you're going to kill it. This lets us know that Jesus is saying, "Don't go for a temporary solution. Kill unforgiveness and bitterness in your life by commanding them to be planted in the sea, and they will *obey* you."

This word "obey" is the Greek word *hupakouo*, which is a compound of the words *hupo* and *akouo*. The word *hupo* means *under*, and *akouo* means *to hear*. When we put these words together to form *hupakouo*, it means *to be in submission or obedience to what is spoken*. When bitterness and unforgiveness hear your voice of authority telling them to shut up and be planted in the sea, they have to submit and obey you, because you carry Christ's authority by coming under His authority.

Friend, don't let offense lodge in your heart and turn into bitterness and unforgiveness. Close the door to the enemy and the sickness and weakness he wants to bring into your life. Make the choice to forgive, and God will empower you. Speak to bitterness and unforgiveness in your heart and demand they be uprooted and planted in the sea, and they will obey you.

STUDY QUESTIONS

Study to shew thyself approved unto God, a workman that needeth not to be ashamed, rightly dividing the word of truth.
— 2 Timothy 2:15

1. How important is it for you to forgive those who mistreat and hurt you? Read these passages from God's Word and write what the Holy Spirit shows you:
   - Matthew 6:14,15; Mark 11:25
   - Ephesians 4:32; Colossians 3:12-14
   - Matthew 18:21-35
2. Of all the facts about the sycamine tree, which one(s) amazed you most? Why? How do these facts help you see unforgiveness and bitterness differently and move you to deal with them quickly?
3. Forgiving someone is not natural — it's *super*natural. Therefore, to truly forgive and keep on forgiving those who offend and hurt us, we need the supernatural power of God, which He calls *grace*. According to First Peter 5:5 and James 4:6, what heart attitude do we need in order to receive God's grace? How is pursuing peace with others connected to receiving God's grace?

PRACTICAL APPLICATION

But be ye doers of the word, and not hearers only, deceiving your own selves.
— James 1:22

1. Friend, receiving communion is a very meaningful, weighty thing that matters deeply to God. It's an expression that honors our covenant with Him and His people, and we should never partake of it haphazardly. Before you take communion, take time to seriously examine yourself to see if you're honoring your covenant with God and His Church. Repent of anything that you know is keeping you from having a clear conscience before God and living in unity with others.

When you do this, you can partake of communion with confidence that Jesus' life will fill and supernaturally empower you to fulfill the calling He's given you.

2. Do you know if you're offended with someone? Take time now to pray: *Holy Spirit, I invite You to search my heart thoroughly and show me any unforgiveness or bitterness I'm holding on to toward anyone* (*see* Psalm 139:23,24). If the Lord brings someone to mind, simply follow these steps:

- Ask God to forgive you for holding on to unforgiveness toward (person's name).
- Release them into God's hands to deal with when and how He chooses (He's the Judge).
- Ask God to heal the hurts and wounds they caused in your heart and soul.
- With God's help, pray a prayer of blessing over the person who hurt you (*see* 1 Peter 3:8,9).
- Repeat these steps whenever the enemy brings this offense back to your mind.

Remember, forgiveness is not letting the person who hurt you off the hook; it's setting you free and placing them in God's hands to deal with and take vengeance as He sees fit. Likewise, forgiveness is not a feeling; it's **a repeated decision** not to rehearse what they did or how you feel about it, but to forgive them and pray God's best for them.

LESSON 4

TOPIC

Not Putting an End to Worry

SCRIPTURES

1. **Isaiah 53:4,5** — Surely he hath borne our griefs, and carried our sorrows: yet we did esteem him stricken, smitten of God, and afflicted. But he was wounded for our transgressions, he was bruised for our iniquities: the chastisement of our peace was upon him; and with his stripes we are healed.

2. **1 Peter 5:8** — Be sober, be vigilant; because your adversary the devil, as a roaring lion, walketh about, seeking whom he may devour.
3. **Matthew 6:25** — Therefore I say unto you, Take no thought for your life, what ye shall eat, or what ye shall drink; nor yet for your body, what shall ye put on. Is not the life more than meat, and the body than raiment?
4. **Philippians 4:6** — Be careful for nothing; but in every thing by prayer and supplication with thanksgiving let your requests be made known unto God.
5. **James 5:16** — …The effectual fervent prayer of a righteous man availeth much.
6. **Philippians 4:7** — And the peace of God, which passeth all understanding, shall keep your hearts and minds through Christ Jesus.

GREEK WORDS

1. "sober" — νήφω (*nepho*): to be sober, not drunk; to think straight, not like a silly drunk
2. "vigilant" — γρηγορέω (*gregoreo*): to put up one's guard against a sinister outside force or enemy
3. "devour" — καταπίνω (*katapino*): to drink or swallow down; to gulp; to slurp; to devour
4. "thought" — μεριμνάω (*merimnao*): to be troubled, anxious, or fretful; primarily used in connection with worry about finances, hunger, or some other basic provision needed for life
5. "careful" — μεριμνάω (*merimnao*): to be troubled, anxious, or fretful; primarily used in connection with worry about finances, hunger, or some other basic provision needed for life
6. "nothing" — μηδέν (*meden*): absolutely nothing
7. "prayer" — προσευχή (*proseuche*): the most common word for prayer in the New Testament; a compound of the words πρός (*pros*) and εὔχομαι (*euchomai*); the word πρός (*pros*) is a preposition that means toward, and denotes closeness; the word εὔχομαι (*euchomai*) describes a wish, desire, prayer, or vow; compounded, to draw near to make an exchange
8. "supplication" — δέησις (*deisis*): a person who has some type of lack in his life and who strongly requests for his lack to be met
9. "thanksgiving" — εὐχαριστία (*eucharistia*): an outpouring of a heart full of grace and feelings that freely flow from the heart

10. "requests" — **αἰτέω** (*aiteo*): to be adamant in requesting assistance to meet tangible needs, such as food, shelter, money, and so forth
11. "known" — **γνωρίζω** (*gnoridzo*): to make a thing known; to declare something; to broadcast something; or to make something very evident
12. "passeth" — **ὑπερέχω** (*huperecho*): the first part of the word is **ὑπέρ** (*huper*), and it means over, above, and beyond; depicts something that is way beyond measure; the idea of superiority; something that is utmost, paramount, foremost, first-rate, first-class, and top-notch; greater, higher, and better than; superior to; preeminent, dominant, and incomparable; more than a match for; unsurpassed or unequaled
13. "understanding" — **νοῦς** (*nous*): the mind; pictures the mind and emotions
14. "keep" — **φρουρέω** (*phroureo*): the idea of soldiers who stood faithfully at their post at the city gates to guard and control all who went in and out of the city; soldiers who served as gate monitors, and no one entered or exited the city without their approval

SYNOPSIS

Is it God's will for you to be healthy and whole? The answer is *yes*. He said in His Word, "Beloved, I wish above all things that thou mayest prosper and be in health, even as thy soul prospereth" (3 John 2). This leads us to ask the primary question we've been focusing on in this series, which is *Why do Christians get sick?*

So far, we have seen three primary causes for sickness in the lives of believers: (1) Many Christians become ill because they don't realize physical healing is provided through Jesus' atonement, (2) a number of Christians get sick because they don't take time to rest, and (3) believers that haven't dealt with bitterness and unforgiveness open the door for sickness and disease to enter their lives.

Another major cause of poor health and sickness is not letting go of worry and genuinely trusting God to care for us. Indeed, modern science confirms that those who worry are much more prone to develop stress-related health struggles. In this lesson, we will explore five steps to move us out of worry and into faith provided by Paul in Philippians 4:6.

The emphasis of this lesson:

Another major reason Christians get sick is worrying. Left unchecked, worry will devour your joy, your peace, and even your health. God wants you to stop worrying and cast your concerns on Him. Rather than worry, get close to God and pray. Boldly ask for the specific things you need and thank Him in advance for answering you. When you do, His peace will guard your heart and mind, shutting out all anxiety, fear, and worry.

A REVIEW OF OUR ANCHOR VERSES
Isaiah 53:4,5

The promise of healing and wholeness is established in the atoning work of Jesus. Writing under the inspiration of the Holy Spirit, the prophet Isaiah predicted that the Messiah — Jesus Christ — would suffer and pay the price for our redemption as well as our physical healing. He said, "Surely he hath borne our griefs, and carried our sorrows: yet we did esteem him stricken, smitten of God, and afflicted" (Isaiah 53:4).

The word "surely" is the Hebrew word *aken*, and it means *indeed, definitely, categorically*, or *emphatically*. Without question, Isaiah said, "Jesus hath borne our griefs." The Hebrew word for "griefs" describes *sicknesses, diseases*, and *physical infirmities of all kinds*; it cannot be translated any other way.

Jesus also has "…carried our sorrows…" (Isaiah 53:4). The word "carried" means *to bear a heavy load*, and the word "sorrows" carries the idea of *physical or mental pain*. Hence, the heavy load of our physical pain and mental torment was laid upon Jesus.

Isaiah went on to say, "But he was wounded for our transgressions, he was bruised for our iniquities…" (Isaiah 53:5). The word "transgressions" has everything to do with our *sin* and *rebellion against God*, and the word "iniquities" is the Hebrew word signifying *guilt* and *shame*. Jesus was "wounded" and "bruised" to pay the penalty for our sin and eradicate guilt and shame from our lives.

Next, the verse says, "…The chastisement of our peace was upon him…" (Isaiah 53:5). The word "peace" here is the marvelous Hebrew word *shalom*, which describes *wholeness and completeness in every area of our life*, including our health. Furthermore, Scripture tells us, "…with his stripes we are healed" (Isaiah 53:5). In Hebrew, this word "healed" is *rapha*, and it emphatically describes *physical healing*. Jesus received "stripes" — *physical blows that inflicted bruises and black and blue marks* on His body — in order for us to be healed, totally cured of all diseases and disorders.

To be clear: The word *healed* does *not* describe "spiritual healing" — there is no such thing. Before we were saved, we were spiritually dead in sin. Through the finished work of Jesus, the Spirit of God resurrected us from spiritual death and has totally annihilated all forms of disease and sickness that come against our body, mind, and emotions. If you're a Christian and you're sick in body or soul, please realize that Jesus has paid the price to heal you and make you whole. Praise His Name forever!

The Enemy Is Out to Devour You

Another major reason Christians get sick is worrying. Left unchecked, worry will devour our joy, our peace, and even our health. First Peter 5:8 says, "Be sober, be vigilant; because your adversary the devil, as a roaring lion, walketh about, seeking whom he may devour." The word "sober" here is the Greek word *nepho*, which means *to be sober, not drunk*. It carries the idea of thinking straight, not like someone who's intoxicated.

In addition to being sober, the Bible says we're to be "vigilant." This is the Greek word *gregoreo*, and it means *to put up one's guard against a sinister outside force or enemy that's trying to get in*. Thus, we are to *think straight, not like a disoriented drunk* and *be on high alert because the devil is trying to gain access to our lives*.

The word "devil" in Greek is *diabolos*, which is more of his job description than name. It describes *one who hits and strikes repeatedly against a person's mind trying to penetrate and totally scramble their thoughts*. That's what the devil does. He roams around like a roaring lion, seeking whom he may devour. This word "devour" is the Greek word *katapino*, a compound of the words *kata* and *pino*. The word *kata* means *down*, and the word *pino* means *to eat or drink*. When these two words are joined to form *katapino*, it means *to drink or swallow down, to gulp, to slurp*, or *to devour*.

This lets us know that the devil's intention is not just to chew on us a little bit and then leave us alone. On the contrary, he wants to completely devour us until there's nothing left but the blood, and then he wants to slurp that up as well. Worry is a major way the devil works his way into a person's life to systematically devour them.

God Said 'Stop Worrying' and Let Me Care for You

Jesus knew the life-draining, sickness-inducing effects of worry. At the same time, He knew the faithfulness of our heavenly Father who loves us without measure and desires to meet our needs. That is why He said, "Therefore I say unto you, Take no thought for your life, what ye shall eat, or what ye shall drink; nor yet for your body, what shall ye put on. Is not the life more than meat, and the body than raiment?" (Matthew 6:25).

The word "thought" in this verse is the Greek word *merimnao*, which means *to be troubled, anxious, or fretful*. This term is primarily used in connection with *worry about finances, hunger*, or *some other basic provision needed for life*. In this verse, however, it is joined with the little Greek prefix *me*, which is *a strong prohibition to stop something that is already in progress*. Essentially, Jesus is urging His listeners to stop worrying, which means the verse could be translated, "Stop worrying about your life...."

What's interesting is that Jesus used the same word here as Paul used in Philippians 4:6, where he said, "Be careful for nothing; but in every thing by prayer and supplication with thanksgiving let your requests be made known unto God." The word "careful" here is again the word *merimnao*, which means *to be troubled, anxious, or fretful* and was primarily used in connection with *worry about finances, hunger*, or *some other basic provision needed for life*.

The apostle Paul's use of this word depicts...

- A person who is fretful about paying his bills
- A person who is worried he won't have the money to purchase food or clothes for his family
- A person who is worried he can't pay his house payment or apartment rent on time
- Any person anxious about his ability to cope with the daily necessities of life

In this verse, Paul was pleading with believers not to worry about the basic needs and provisions required for life. Likewise, he was telling them not to let the events of life get to them or throw them into a state of anxiety or panic. Instead, Paul wrote, "Be careful for nothing..." (Philippians 4:6). In

Greek, the word "nothing" is a translation of the word *meden*, which means *absolutely nothing*.

Taking into account the original Greek meaning, here is the *Renner Interpretive Version* (*RIV*) of this portion of Philippians 4:6:

Don't worry about anything — and that means nothing at all!

5 Steps to Move Out of Worry and Into Faith

Paul then goes on to write, "…But in every thing by prayer and supplication with thanksgiving let your requests be made known unto God" (Philippians 4:6). Here we find five specific things we can do to walk away from worry and into faith. These include *prayer, supplication, thanksgiving, requests*, and the last one is connected to the word *known*.

STEP 1: **PRAYER.** The word "prayer" in Philippians 4:6 is a translation of the Greek word *proseuche*, which is the most common word for *prayer* in the New Testament. It is a compound of the words *pros* and *euchomai*. The word *pros* is a preposition that means *toward*, and denotes *closeness*; the word *euchomai* describes *a wish, desire, prayer*, or *vow*. When these words are compounded to form *proseuche*, it pictures *one who draws near to God in order to make an exchange*.

Instead of carrying our worries and our burdens, Paul tells us to *get close to the Lord* in prayer and give Him our worries, fears, and concerns. In exchange, He will give us His *peace*, which we'll look at more closely in a few moments.

STEP 2: **SUPPLICATION.** The next thing Paul lists is "supplication," which is a translation of the Greek word *deisis*. It pictures *a person who has some type of lack in his life and who strongly requests for it to be met*. In fact, he is in such great need that he pushes his pride out of the way so he can boldly, earnestly, strongly, and passionately ask someone to help him.

One of the most powerful examples of the word *deisis* is found in James 5:16, which says, "…The effectual fervent prayer of a righteous man availeth much." Here the word *deisis* is translated as "fervent prayer." It depicts coming to God on the most serious terms to strongly ask Him to meet a specific need you're praying about or facing in your life. The use of this word *deisis* means *you can get very bold* when you ask God to move on your behalf.

There is no reason for you to be timid or mealy-mouthed when you pray. You can tell God *exactly* what you feel, what you're facing, and what you need Him to do. This is what "supplication" is all about!

STEP 3: **THANKSGIVING**. God not only expects you to be bold, He also wants you to *thank Him* in advance for answering you. We are even told to enter His presence by expressing "thanksgiving" (*see* Psalm 100:4). This word "thanksgiving" in Philippians 4:6 is the Greek word *eucharistia*, which is a compound of the words *eu* and *charis*. The word *eu* describes *something swell* or *really wonderful*, and the word *charis* is the Greek word for *grace*. When compounded, the new word *eucharistia* depicts *an outpouring of a heart full of grace and feelings that freely flow from the heart to God.*

The use of this word indicates that when we earnestly ask God to do something for us, we should match it with an earnest outpouring of thanks. Thanking Him in advance demonstrates faith, so make sure to follow up your earnest asking with earnest thanksgiving! It will change the atmosphere of your heart and stoke your hope and anticipation of how He will answer.

STEP 4: **REQUESTS**. Again, Paul said, "…But in every thing by prayer and supplication with thanksgiving let your *requests* be made known unto God" (Philippians 4:6). This word "requests" is a translation of the Greek word *aiteo*, which means *to be adamant in requesting assistance to meet tangible needs*, such as *food, shelter, money, and so forth.*

This word *aiteo* — translated here as "requests" — expresses the idea that *a person has a full expectation to receive what was requested*. This person knows what he needs and is so filled with faith that he isn't afraid to boldly ask and expect to receive what he has requested. This means when you pray about a need that concerns you, pray authoritatively — knowing that you have the right as His child to ask and expecting Him to honor His Word and do what you have requested.

STEP 5: **KNOWN**. Notice that Paul said, "…Let your requests be made *known* unto God" (Philippians 4:6), the word "known" is the unusual Greek word *gnoridzo*, which means *to make a thing known* or *to declare something*. One expositor of Scripture has said it means *to broadcast something* or *to make something very evident.*

So when we make our requests "known" to God, we declare to Him what we need, broadcasting it so loudly that all of Heaven hears you when you pray. You can be bold when you make your requests known to God!

Taking into account all the original Greek meanings, here is the *Renner Interpretive Version* (*RIV*) of Philippians 4:6:

> **Don't worry about anything — and that means nothing at all! Instead, come before God and give Him the things that concern you so He can in exchange give you what you need or desire. Be bold to strongly, passionately, and fervently make your request known to God, making certain that an equal measure of thanksgiving goes along with your strong asking. You have every right to ask boldly, so go ahead and insist that God meet your need. When you pray, be so bold that there is no doubt your prayer was heard. Broadcast it! Declare it! Pray boldly with the assurance that God has heard your request.**

You Can Have Peace That Overrides Logic

When you don't worry about anything and pray about everything, boldly declaring and broadcasting your tangible needs to God — with an earnest amount of thanksgiving — Scripture says, "And the peace of God, which passeth all understanding, shall keep your hearts and minds through Christ Jesus" (Philippians 4:7).

Notice the word "passeth." In Greek, it is the word *huperecho*, which is a compound of the words *huper* and *echo*. The word *huper* means *over, above, and beyond*, and it depicts *something that is way beyond measure*. It is the idea of *superiority*; something that is *utmost, paramount, foremost, first-rate, first-class*, and *top-notch*. It means *greater, higher*, and *better than*; *superior to*; *preeminent, dominant*, and *incomparable*; *more than a match for*; and *unsurpassed or unequaled*. All these words describe the kind of God-peace you will receive as you pray instead of worry.

In Philippians 4:7, Paul said, "…[It's] the peace of God, which passeth all understanding…." The word "understanding" is a form of the Greek word *nous*, which is the term for *the mind* and pictures *the mind and emotions*. When we worry, we're struggling in our mind and emotions, and this verse tells us that when we pray and thank God, His peace will come and calm our hearts and minds.

And Paul went on to write, God's peace "...shall keep your hearts and minds through Christ Jesus" (Philippians 4:7). The word "keep" here is quite amazing. It is the Greek word *phroureo*, a word that is exclusively used to describe *soldiers who stood faithfully at their post at the city gates to guard and control all who went in and out of the city*. These warriors served as gate monitors, and no one entered or exited the city without their approval. This tells us that when we follow the instruction of Philippians 4:6 — praying about everything instead of worrying — God's peace will be released and stand as a guardian at the gates of our hearts and minds, determining what gets in and what is denied entrance.

Taking into account the original Greek meaning, here is the *Renner Interpretive Version (RIV)* of Philippians 4:7:

> **And the peace of God — a peace that rises far above and goes beyond anything the human mind could ever think, reason, imagine, or produce by itself — will stand at the entrance of your heart and mind like a guard to control, monitor, and screen everything that tries to access your mind, heart, and emotions.**

Friend, believe God when He says worry is a waste of your time that will not help one bit. Make the choice today to slam the door in the enemy's face by developing the habit of turning to God in prayer instead of worrying. God is faithful to hear and answer your requests, and in the meantime He will give you His peace to protect your mind and heart and snuff out fear in all its forms.

STUDY QUESTIONS

> Study to shew thyself approved unto God, a workman that needeth not to be ashamed, rightly dividing the word of truth.
> — 2 Timothy 2:15

1. Have you ever struggled with worry? What are some of the biggest issues on your mind right now? Pray and ask the Holy Spirit to show you any fearful thinking that is fueling worry. Surrender any fears to Him and ask Him to help you *reframe* how you see the situations using specific scriptures of hope and victory. Consider these promises God has made to you:

- Matthew 6:25-34; Luke 12:22-32
- Romans 8:31; Psalm 34:9,10; 84:11
- Philippians 4:6-8; 1 Peter 5:7
- Hebrews 13:5,6

2. Looking back at the original definition of "devil" (*diabolos*), it's easier to see that the enemy's strategy is to intoxicate you with worrisome thoughts so you're too overwhelmed to fight back. In your own words, list the 5 steps to move out of worry and into faith from Philippians 4:6 and give a brief description of each.

3. One of the greatest scriptures about peace is found in **Colossians 3:15**. Take time to meditate on this verse in the *Amplified* version and allow God's peace to find permanent residency inside of you.

And let the peace (soul harmony which comes) from Christ rule (act as umpire continually) in your hearts [deciding and settling with finality all questions that arise in your minds, in that peaceful state] to which as [members of Christ's] one body you were also called [to live]. And be thankful (appreciative), [giving praise to God always].

PRACTICAL APPLICATION

But be ye doers of the word, and not hearers only, deceiving your own selves.
—James 1:22

1. What is an area of your life where going to God in prayer comes more naturally? What do you find it hard to pray about? Ask the Holy Spirit to show you the reasons behind both answers and to give you the strength (grace) to grow in your ability to trust Him and speak freely with Him regarding all areas of your life.

2. Imagine for a moment what it would be like to be genuinely free from worry. With the peace of God calling the shots in your mind and emotions — and anxiety and fear kept out — what would your life be like? What would you be able to do? Which situations would you be able to approach without fear? This is the kind of life God wants you to live! Take a moment to pray:

Lord, forgive me for worrying about so many things. Help me recognize the roots of wrong, fearful thinking and uproot them and replant right thinking with the truth of Your Word. Help me find a verse for every victory I need and begin to pray about everything rather than worry. In Jesus' name. Amen!

LESSON 5

TOPIC
Not Taking Good Care of Your Temple

SCRIPTURES

1. **Isaiah 53:4,5** — Surely he hath borne our griefs, and carried our sorrows: yet we did esteem him stricken, smitten of God, and afflicted. But he was wounded for our transgressions, he was bruised for our iniquities: the chastisement of our peace was upon him; and with his stripes we are healed.
2. **1 Corinthians 6:19,20** — What? know ye not that your body is the temple of the Holy Ghost which is in you, which ye have of God, and ye are not your own? For ye are bought with a price: therefore glorify God in your body, and in your spirit, which are God's.
3. **Genesis 2:8,15** — And the Lord God planted a garden eastward in Eden; and there he put the man whom he had formed.... And the Lord God took the man, and put him into the garden of Eden to dress it and to keep it.
4. **1 Thessalonians 4:4** — That every one of you should know [of himself] how to possess his vessel in sanctification and honour.
5. **1 Corinthians 10:31** — Whether therefore ye eat, or drink, or whatsoever ye do, do all to the glory of God.
6. **1 Corinthians 9:27** — But I keep under my body, and bring it into subjection....
7. **1 Timothy 4:8** — For bodily exercise profiteth little....

GREEK WORDS

1. "what" — ἤ (*e*): an exclamation

2. "know ye not" — οὐκ οἴδατε (*ouk oidate*): from οὐκ (*ouk*) and οἶδα (*oida*); the word οὐκ (*ouk*) is an emphatic no, and οἶδα (*oida*) means to comprehend; the word οἶδα (*oida*) depicts knowledge gained by personal experience or personal observation; in this verse, have you not emphatically comprehended
3. "that" — ὅτι (*hoti*): points to an important point
4. "body" — σῶμα (*soma*): the physical body
5. "temple" — ναός (*naos*): a temple or a highly decorated shrine; the image of vaulted ceilings, marble, granite, gold, silver, and highly decorated ornamentation; the most innermost part of a temple; holy of holies
6. "in" — ἐν (*en*): literally, in or inside
7. "ye have" — ἔχω (*echo*): to have, hold, or possess
8. "of" — ἀπό (*apo*): from, as directly from God
9. "not your own" — οὐκ ἐστὲ ἑαυτῶν (*ouk este heauton*): "emphatically not your own"
10. "bought" — ἀγοράζω (*agoradzo*): used to denote the purchase of a slave out of the slave market; to redeem
11. "price" — τιμή (*time*): price; value; worth; a price that is costly and extremely valuable; literally, at a great price
12. "therefore" — δή (*de*): consequently; subsequently
13. "possess" — κτάομαι (*ktaomai*): to control, manage, or win the mastery over; personal mastery; implying you should master your body and your body should not master you
14. "vessel" — σκεῦος (*skeuos*): a utensil, like a tool, a utensil in the kitchen, but here depicts the human body
15. "sanctification" — ἁγιασμός (*hagiasmos*): to treat something as holy, consecrated, sacred; from ἅγιος (*hagios*), holy
16. "honor" — τιμή (*time*): price; value; worth; a price that is costly and extremely valuable
17. "keep under" — ὑπωπιάζω (*hupopiadzo*): describes the area of face below the eyes
18. "bodily exercise" — σωματικὴ γυμνασία (*somatike gumnasia*): the word σῶμα (*soma*) depicts the human body, and γυμνασία (*gumnasia*) is from γυμνάζω (*gumnadzo*), naked athletes who exercised with no hinderances
19. "profits" — ὠφέλιμος (*ophelimos*): a moral obligation

SYNOPSIS

The topic we've been focusing on is *Why Christians Get Sick and How They Can Become Healthy Again*. In our first lesson, we saw one of the most common reasons many Christians get sick is simply because they don't know that healing is in the atonement — or finished work — of Jesus. In our second lesson, we learned that Christians also get sick because they don't honor the Sabbath and never take time to rest and refresh themselves. In Lesson 3, we focused on the deadly snare of unforgiveness and bitterness, which result from not dealing with offense. For many believers, this is a major door-opener to disease and health disorders of all kinds. Then in our last lesson, we discovered that Christians often get sick because they're stuck in a habit of worrying instead of praying and making their requests known to God.

What else can make us susceptible to sickness and disease? The answer is not taking good care of our body, which is the temple of the Holy Spirit. Although we may not want to hear it, what we eat and our commitment to exercise are two important issues that can make or break the quality of our life. With God's help we can develop a personal plan that is blessed by God to pursue and experience health in our body and soul.

The emphasis of this lesson:

Your body is the temple of the Holy Spirit. You have been redeemed by the precious blood of Jesus, and you're not your own. God calls you to glorify Him in your body by taking care of and maintaining it. This includes eating healthy foods and exercising regularly. Although the benefits of exercise are temporary, the Bible says you have an absolute duty to do it.

A FINAL REVIEW OF OUR ANCHOR VERSES

Isaiah 53:4,5

The biblical foundation for our physical healing is clearly seen in Isaiah's prophecy concerning our suffering Messiah. In this well-known passage, the Hebrew language emphatically declares that Jesus paid the price for our physical as well as mental healing. Isaiah 53:4 says, "Surely he hath borne our griefs, and carried our sorrows: yet we did esteem him stricken, smitten of God, and afflicted."

"Surely" — the Hebrew word *aken* — means *categorically, indeed, truly,* or *definitely.* Without question, Jesus has borne our "griefs."

"Griefs" — the Hebrew word *choli* — can only be translated as *sicknesses, diseases,* or *illnesses.* Thus, Jesus carried all our physical infirmities and carried our "sorrows."

"Sorrows" — the Hebrew word *makob* — from a verb meaning to be *in physical or mental pain.* On the Cross, Jesus paid the price for us to be free from mental anguish and sickness as well as physical infirmities. Isaiah went on to say, "…He was wounded for our transgressions…" (Isaiah 53:5).

"Wounded" — the Hebrew word *chalal* — means *pierced* or *wounded* and refers to *the piercing of Jesus' hands, feet, and side.*

"Transgressions" — the Hebrew word *pesha* —describes *sin, transgression, rebellion,* or *revolt.* Not only did Jesus take upon His body the punishment for our sin, He was also "…bruised for our iniquities…" (Isaiah 53:5).

"Iniquities" — the Hebrew word *avon* — primarily has to do with *guilt* and *shame.* Jesus was "bruised" — *crushed* and *beaten to pieces* — to eradicate guilt and shame from our lives. What's more, "…The chastisement of our peace was upon him…" (Isaiah 53:5).

"Peace" — the Hebrew word *shalom* — describes *wholeness* and *completeness* in every area of our life. This includes *health, happiness, prosperity, safety, security, soundness,* and *overall welfare.* Isaiah then declared, "…With his [Jesus'] stripes we are healed" (Isaiah 53:5).

"Healed" — the Hebrew word *rapha* — means *to heal* and describes *physical healing of defects, illnesses,* and *sicknesses.* It is also the word used for *a physician.* Jesus received "stripes" — *blows, bruises,* and *black and blue marks* — in His physical body so we could receive physical healing from all illnesses.

Clearly, the words in these verses emphatically declare that Jesus carried our sicknesses, our illnesses, and our mental problems so we wouldn't have to. He also dealt a deathblow to our sin and took upon Himself our guilt and shame. In return, He gave us peace — wholeness and completeness in every area of our lives.

Your Body Is God's Temple

Did you know that your physical body is the home of the Holy Spirit? In **First Corinthians 6:19**, the apostle Paul wrote to the Corinthian believers because they were living and behaving way below God's holy standards. Out of shock over the reports that had reached his ears, Paul said,

> **What? know ye not that your body is the temple of the Holy Ghost which is in you, which ye have of God, and ye are not your own?**

Notice the first word of this verse — the word "what." In Greek, it is actually *an exclamation*. It is the equivalent of Paul saying, "What! What is this? I don't understand." He then added the phrase, "Know ye not," which in Greek is *ouk oidate*. The word *ouk* is *an emphatic no*, and the word *oidate* is from the word *oida*, which means *to understand or comprehend*. When you put all these words together, Paul was essentially saying, "What's this? Do you not yet understand? Do you really not get it? Have you not realized *that*...."

Even the word "that" is important. It's the Greek word *hoti*, and it indicates *the important point* Paul is making. He said, "What? know ye not **that** *your body is the temple of the Holy Ghost*...?" (1 Corinthians 6:19). He really wanted them — and *us* — to understand *that* their bodies were God's temple. In Greek, the word "body" is the word *soma*, and it refers to *the physical body*. The fact that our body becomes God's temple is truly a miracle. The moment we surrender our life to Jesus, God swoops in and transforms our physical body into a divine container of the Holy Spirit. You are His *temple*.

The word "temple" in this verse is the Greek word *naos*, and it describes *a temple* or *a highly decorated shrine*. It paints a picture of vaulted ceilings, marble, granite, gold, silver, and highly decorated ornamentation. Furthermore, it depicts *the most sacred, innermost part of a temple* and is the very word used in the Old Testament Septuagint to describe *the Holy of Holies*.

If Jesus is your Lord and Savior, then the Holy Spirit has moved inside of you and become a permanent resident in your life. You are now a walking, breathing sanctuary. That's what Paul was communicating to the

Corinthians and to us, when he said, "...Your body is the temple of the Holy Ghost which is *in* you..." (1 Corinthians 6:19).

The word "in" here is the Greek word *en*, and it specifically identifies the location where the Holy Spirit is — *inside* us. Paul then added, "...which ye have of God..." (1 Corinthians 6:19). The words "ye have" is a form of the Greek word *echo*, which means *to have, to hold, to possess*, or *to contain*. Essentially, Paul was saying, "We are the *holders*, the *possessors*, or the *containers* of this remarkable gift which we have "of God." The word "of" here is the Greek word *apo*, and it means *directly from God*. The transformation we experienced the day we were saved is not a result of personal rehabilitation or reform. It is something we received as a gift directly from God.

Paul goes on to say, "...Ye are not your own. For ye are bought with a price..." (1 Corinthians 6:19,20). The words "not your own" in Greek mean *emphatically not your own*, and the word "bought" is the Greek word *agoradzo*, which is the term for *redemption* and was used to denote *the purchase of a slave out of the slave market*. The Bible says we were redeemed for a "price." This word "price" is the Greek word *time*, and it means *price, value*, or *worth*. It describes *that which is costly and extremely valuable* and literally means *at a great price*. The indescribable cost for our redemption was the blood of Jesus. Because of the marvelous work of His grace in our lives, we are not our own anymore. Our body, soul, and spirit belong to Him who loved us and gave Himself for us.

'Glorify' God in Your Body

Knowing that we were purchased by the blood of Jesus, Paul said, "...Therefore glorify God in your body, and in your spirit, which are God's" (1 Corinthians 6:20). The word "therefore" is the little Greek word *de*, which means *consequently* or s*ubsequently*. Basically, Paul said, "As a result of and in response to what Jesus did, glorify God in your body and in your spirit."

The word "glorify" is the Greek word *doxadzo*, which is a form of the word *dokeo*, and it means *to think* or *to estimate*. The use of this word lets us know that in order to glorify God, we really need to *put our minds to it*. We can't be halfhearted about it or just hope it happens. We have to strongly consider the value, the weight, and the worth of how we can best bring

God glory in our "body," which again is the Greek word *soma*, the term for the *physical body*.

Most believers focus solely on glorifying God in their *spirit*, and while that is certainly included in First Corinthians 6:20, we are also instructed to glorify Him in our *body*. When Jesus died, He redeemed both our spirit and our body. Therefore, it is no longer ours but His, and He wants us to make a well thought-out decision of how we can best glorify Him with it — it is His temple after all.

This principle of taking good care of what God has entrusted to us was established back at the beginning of creation. The Bible says, "And the Lord God took the man, and put him into the garden of Eden to dress it and to keep it" (Genesis 2:15). Even though Eden was a perfect paradise, God still placed Adam in charge of it and told him to dress it and keep it. The words "dress it" carry the idea of *cultivating something*, and the phrase "keep it" means *to guard and protect something*. In the same way, God has placed us in charge of our physical body, and He wants us to develop it as well as guard and protect it. That is how we "glorify God with our body."

Learn to Manage Your Body in 'Sanctification and Honor'

Consider what Paul says in First Thessalonians 4:4: "That every one of you should know how to possess his vessel in sanctification and honour." What's interesting about this verse is that in the original Greek, there are two words that don't appear in the *King James Version*. It actually says, "That every one of you should know *of himself* how to possess his vessel in sanctification and honour" (1 Thessalonians 4:4). This means each of us has to become familiar with our own self and know how to "possess his vessel."

The word "possess" in this verse is the Greek word *ktaomai*, which means *to control*, *manage*, or *win the mastery over*. It clearly depicts *personal mastery* and implies that you should master your body and your body should not master you. Here, Paul calls the physical body a "vessel" — using the Greek word *skeuos* — which is the word for *a utensil in the kitchen* or *a tool in the toolbox*. Specifically, it is used here to depict the human body as an *instrument* in God's hands.

How are we to manage and master our body? Paul said "...in sanctification and honour" (1 Thessalonians 4:4). The word "sanctification" is the

Greek word *hagiasmos*, which means *to treat something as holy, consecrated, or sacred*. It's taken from the word *hagios*, the word for *holy*. We are also to treat our body in "honor," which is the Greek word *time*, describing *price, value*, or *worth*. In this case, it particularly signifies *a price that is costly and extremely valuable*. Again, we have been redeemed out of Satan's control by the precious blood of Jesus, and that makes us *holy* and *priceless* in God's eyes. Therefore, what He calls holy and priceless, we need to call holy and priceless and treat it as such.

If you don't take care of and maintain your physical body, it will end up broken, in pain, or out of commission. You need the right kind of daily nourishment, regular exercise, and proper hygiene in order to master your body and keep it in good shape. Just sitting or lying around watching TV, surfing the internet, or playing computer games is a surefire way to develop health problems. You have to make a decision that you're going to master yourself and keep your body active and moving so you don't lose its functionality. As the old saying goes, if you don't use it, you'll lose it. Therefore, you need to develop a plan to keep your body moving in ways that you enjoy and work well for you.

How's Your Eating?

Stop and think: *What kinds of foods am I putting into my body? Are they healthy and full of life? Or are they processed and empty of nutrition?* This is not meant to condemn you in any way, as all of us could probably come up higher in this area. To a great degree, what you eat will determine how you feel and what you're able to do. The apostle Paul gives us a practical yardstick regarding what we eat, what we drink, and everything else we do. He said:

Whether therefore ye eat, or drink, or whatsoever ye do, do all to the glory of God.
— **1 Corinthians 10:31**

Be honest with yourself: Are you eating and drinking to the glory of God? Again, if you're not, please don't feel condemned. This was an area that Rick himself struggled with for quite some time. He candidly shared how he had gained so much weight that he became sick and was struggling just to get around. It got so bad that he and his family were very concerned for his health. Initially, rather than deal with his unhealthy choices, he bought different clothes and dressed in layers to try to hide his true condition.

Finally, he came to the place where he asked himself some hard questions — questions you may want to ask yourself:

- *Am I eating in such a way that brings God glory?*
- *Does my weight glorify God?*
- *Am I just eating out of boredom or am I actually hungry and need nutrition?*
- *Are the things I'm putting in my mouth good for my body?*
- *Can I eat all of these unhealthy foods and enormous portions to the glory of God?*

For Rick, the clear answer to all these questions was a resounding *no*. When God showed him verses like First Corinthians 10:31, he had to repent for not taking care of his body. He then made the decision that he was going to master his body and learn to have healthy discipline and boundaries regarding the food he ate.

"I was the only one that had the power to change what I was doing," Rick said. "Only I could begin to learn how to manage and master myself, and the same is true for you. I had to pray for God's strength every day and then make one intentional decision after another that I was going to change and begin eating and drinking to the glory of God." Again, God's Word says, "Whether therefore ye eat, or drink, or whatsoever ye do, do all to the glory of God" (1 Corinthians 10:31).

Eating to the glory of God is about submitting your diet and your relationship with food to the Lordship of Jesus. Regardless of your weight or size or how out of shape you are, you can turn it around by praying and developing a godly, practical plan and following it. One day at a time — one decision at a time — you can get started and become more mobile than you thought you could be. You'll feel better physically and feel better about yourself emotionally. You may even be able to get off many of the medications you've been on once your doctor gives you the go-ahead!

Are You Exercising?

Another area that Rick really had to come to grips with was *exercise*. For most people, exercise is something you either love or hate. For Rick, it was virtually nonexistent in his life. Nevertheless, as God got his attention on what he was eating, He also gave him fresh revelation regarding exercise.

One verse of scripture that really helped Rick to make positive changes was First Corinthians 9:27, where Paul said, "But I keep under my body, and bring it into subjection...." The words "keep under" are a translation of the Greek word *hupopiadzo*, and it describes *the area of the face below the eyes*. The one thing located in this region that can often get us in a lot of trouble is our *mouth*. In order to truly bring our body into submission, we have to learn to take authority over our mouth — which includes our appetite.

A second passage that helped Rick but has often been misinterpreted is First Timothy 4:8, which says, "For bodily exercise profiteth little...." Although it appears this verse is downplaying the value of exercise, it actually does not. A closer look at the original meaning of some key words reveals this.

Take, for example, the words "bodily exercise," which are the Greek phrase *somatike gumnasia*. This phrase is a compound of the word *soma* — which is the same word for the *physical body* that we saw in First Corinthians 6:19 — and the word *gumnasia*, which means *exercise* and is where we get the word *gymnasium*. The word *gumnasia* is derived from the Greek word *gumnadzo*, which was used to portray *naked athletes who exercised, trained, and prepared for competition in the athletic games of the ancient world*. Hence the phrase "bodily exercise" carries the idea of *exercising with all of one's might in order to develop oneself*.

As strange as it may seem, removing one's clothes was deemed necessary in the ancient world in order to eliminate all hindrances that otherwise could impede an athlete's movements. Therefore, the use of the word *gumnasia* — translated here as "exercise" — carries the idea of *removing laziness, sluggishness, all excuses, and anything else that would hinder physical movement*. Furthermore, people in the ancient world believed discipline of the body was one of life's chief concerns and that it was essential for physical, mental, and **even spiritual advancement**.

So what does Paul mean when he says bodily exercise "profiteth little"? The key to understanding this lies in knowing the meaning of each of these two words. In Greek, the word "profits" is *ophelimos*, which means *to be morally obligated, to do something as an obligation*, or *to be indebted*. It originally was a legal term to depict one's duty to fulfill obligations. In the context of this verse, it means **we have an absolute duty to exercise**.

This brings us to the word "little," which is the Greek word *oligos*, and it describes *something that is short-lived*. The use of this word tells us that the effects of physical exercise are temporary. Yet, according to First Timothy 4:8, the Holy Spirit is telling us through Paul that **we have a moral obligation and an absolute duty to physically exercise — even though it is only profitable in this temporal life.** When we make a decision to discipline ourselves, strip off laziness and excuses, and develop our physical body, we will also develop ourselves mentally and spiritually.

Now if you're thinking, *Exercise is too difficult for me — I'm too large and I get out of breath after taking a few steps.* That's okay. Surrender yourself to God and start doing something, no matter how small it seems. Some movement is better than no movement. If you can only walk three minutes, walk three minutes. If you get in a pool and just move your arms and legs in the water, do that. The point is *begin to move*. Make a plan and begin to work the plan. Where you start is not where you'll stay. You will improve because God's blessing is on your efforts! And He wants to help you experience better health than you ever thought possible.

Friend, God is for you, not against you, and He doesn't want you to be sick another day. Yes, it may take some time to turn things around, but it will be so incredibly worth it!

STUDY QUESTIONS

> **Study to shew thyself approved unto God, a workman that needeth not to be ashamed, rightly dividing the word of truth.**
> **— 2 Timothy 2:15**

1. Because we were "bought with a price," we are actually not our own anymore. We belong to Jesus, and He calls our body a beautifully decorated *temple* to display His presence and power. How do you care for *your* temple? Is it clean? Is it holy? Is it in disrepair? Do you give much thought or attention to how it's maintained or presented? Take some time to reflect on this powerful instruction from Paul in **Romans 12:1 (*MSG*):**

   So here's what I want you to do, God helping you: Take your everyday, ordinary life — your sleeping, eating, going-to-work, and walking-around life — and place it before God as an offering.

Embracing what God does for you is the best thing you can do for him.

2. How would you describe your relationship with food? Is it a coping mechanism for stress? Do you find yourself afraid to eat too much or too little? Are there certain unhealthy foods you know you're eating too much of? No matter what your answers are, know that **God loves you** and wants to help you have a healthy relationship with food, finding the right balance of nutrients that works best for you. Take some time to meditate on First Corinthians 6:12,13 and 10:23. What is the Holy Spirit showing you in these passages? Are there any adjustments you feel He's asking you to make? If so, what are they?

PRACTICAL APPLICATION

> But be ye doers of the word, and not hearers only, deceiving your own selves.
> —James 1:22

1. In many Christian circles, it can become almost like a badge of honor to be "too busy" to focus on healthy eating and exercise. Oftentimes we can justify not caring for our bodies with the thought, *Well, I'm busy building God's Kingdom and that's more important than meal prepping and working out.* Have you ever fallen into this line of reasoning? What healthy self-care measures have you written off as "unnecessary"?
2. What kind of exercise doesn't feel like a chore to you? Was there a sport or energizing hobby you really enjoyed as a kid or young adult that you haven't gotten to do in a while? If so, what was it, and how can you take baby steps toward making it a part of your life again?
3. If you've never exercised or played sports, what are some activities that sound fun to you? Try some different things to find out what you like and pursue the one(s) that are most enjoyable and work best for you. Finding a fun way to move and be active — and doing it with a friend — is a great way to stay motivated and keep going!

Notes

CLAIM YOUR FREE RESOURCE!

As a way of introducing you further to the teaching ministry of Rick Renner, we would like to send you free of charge his teaching CD, "How To Receive a Miraculous Touch From God."

In His earthly ministry, Jesus commonly healed *all* who were sick of *all* their diseases. In this profound message, learn about the manifold dimensions of Christ's wisdom, goodness, power, and love toward all humanity who came to Him in faith with their needs.

☑ **YES, I want to receive Rick Renner's monthly teaching letter!**

Simply scan the QR code to claim this resource or go to:
renner.org/claim-your-free-offer

Connect WITH US!

- renner.org
- youtube.com/rennerministries
- facebook.com/rickrenner
- instagram.com/rickrrenner